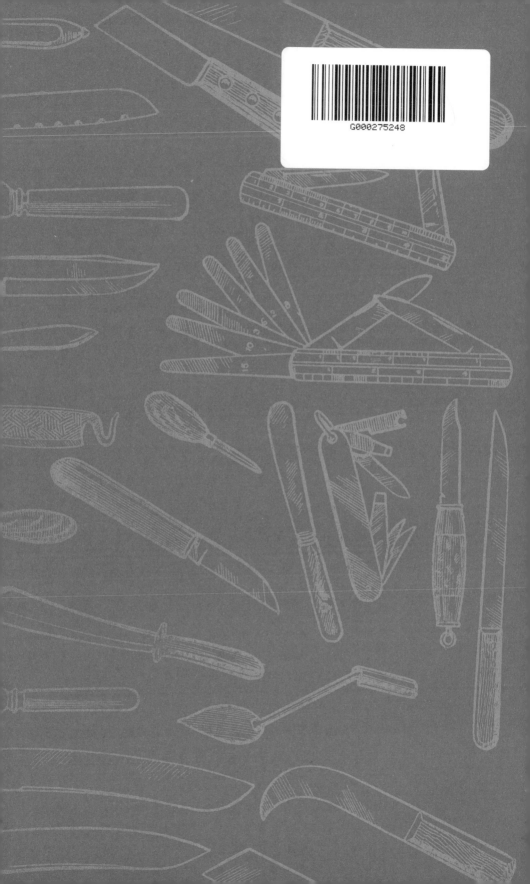

To Marcus

All the best

KNIFE

THE CULTURE, CRAFT AND CULT
OF THE COOK'S KNIFE

TIM HAYWARD

PHOTOGRAPHY BY CHRIS TERRY
SHOKUNIN MANGA BY CHIE KUTSUWADA

quadrille

Publishing Director: Sarah Lavelle
Creative Director: Helen Lewis
Designer: Will Webb
Photographer: Chris Terry
Copy Editor: Simon Davis
Production: Emily Noto and Vincent Smith

First published in 2016 by
Quadrille Publishing
Pentagon House
52–54 Southwark Street
London SE1 1UN
www.quadrille.co.uk

Quadrille is an imprint of Hardie Grant
www.hardiegrant.com.au

Cataloguing in Publication Data: a catalogue record for this book is available
from the British Library.

ISBN: 978 184949 8913

Printed in China

CONTENTS

INTRODUCTION

THERE IS NO OBJECT YOU OWN that is anything like your kitchen knife. Every day you pick it up and use it to create and transform. This, I suppose, could be true of a paintbrush or a keyboard, but the knife is more than a creative or functional tool. Unless, for example, you are a very particular sort of person, the knife will be the only item in your possession designed to cut flesh. Think about it – eight inches of lethally sharp, 'weapons-grade' metal lying on your kitchen table, possessing the same potential for mayhem as a loaded handgun – and yet it is predominantly used to express your love for your family by making their tea.

The knife is one of the few objects to which we give house room while simultaneously fearing. My Old Nan, bless her, 'didn't quite trust' gas and was genuinely relieved when, after the War, she finally 'got The Electric'. I remember my mother quietly disposing of the pressure cooker and the deep-fat fryer as soon as she could. We are a risk-averse populace now and have purged our households of dangerous objects... except the knife. Nor is the knife an easy option: it's the only remaining domestic tool that we must discipline ourselves to master – rather than taking it out of a box, switching it on and expecting it to serve us. Most of us learn from a parent how to use and respect a knife. We commit time and effort to our knives, caring for them, sharpening them, washing them carefully, reverently putting them away in a block, on a rack, in a box. Should we be surprised when what begins as a simple relationship between human and tool so easily elides into a kind of cultist fetishising? What is it about knives that makes us feel this way?

Like most things that we use every day, including our own bodies, a knife will change its shape and functionality over the course of its life. I once sat in a tapas bar in Barcelona and spotted the chef using a knife I'd never seen before. It had a handle like a standard 3-rivet Sabatier but the blade was a wickedly sharp little talon, about an inch long. My Spanish is appalling but I managed to get the owner to explain it. Once, he said, demonstrating with his nicked and burned hands, it had been a six-inch blade, but over 14 years he'd sharpened it down to this... and every working day he used it just to slit the skins from chorizo. There isn't, as far as I'm aware, a 'chorizo peeling knife' in any kitchen supply shop, but there's certainly one behind the bar at Cal Pep. It's knackered, worn, beautiful and it's the child of its owner, its working life and its environment. His knife is a perfect example of *wabi-sabi*, a Japanese word that conveys the aesthetic appeal of something worn and shaped by age and use, the very embodiment of evanescence and acquired 'character'.

The knife is the day-to-day working tool of different craftspeople working with food. Chef's knives are similar to those we keep at home, while the knives of people who cut meat or fish all day are different. Like any craftsman's tools, they are evolved to the work they do and imbued with the spirit of those who work with them. The delicate tourné knife in the hands of a commis chef carving fruit is a million miles from the lethally curved gutting knife in the hands of a trawlerman at sea and yet both have developed, through generations of skilled and specialised use, to share a beautiful simplicity of function.

Because knives are also weapons of war and tools of slaughter they are attended in many cultures by conventions that go so far beyond mere rules that they become taboo. In the West we are used to having knives by our plates but many cultures forbid the presence of something so dangerous at the communal table. It's logical that, in a place where food is shared and hospitality is expressed, there should be no place for a weapon. These conventions go so far back in many cultures that they have affected the entire cuisine.

Our national knife styles can be as unique and individual as national dress or even language. As knives are primarily used in the preparation of food they are as varied as our cuisines and as affected by local ingredients, economies, beliefs and taboos. There is something wonderful in the idea of the knife as a symbol of massive human diversity and, somewhere, I hope that book is being written.

Far more exciting to me than the infinite subtle differences, are the similarities. This book doesn't attempt to be comprehensive. Instead it's a very personal selection of knives from around the world, chosen for the way they represent different physical qualities and how these resonate through the knives of different cultures and cuisines. With so much variety in knives globally it is genuinely a revelation to realise that the human grip is universal, that the ways we have grown to feel we can control the danger of blades* transcend nation and culture. Most exciting is how the design 'responses' of craftsmen throughout history, of every level of skill and artistry, from the shokunin of Japan to a woman making work knives from scrap metal in a market in India, end up so aligned. There must always be a heavy knife; its throat must be deep enough to protect the knuckles in a 'hammer' grip. It takes advantage of weight, whether it's cutting meat in a carnivorous culture or tough vegetables in a vegetarian cuisine. There must always be a knife for cutting towards the thumb; its blade must be narrow, it has no need of a point and the handle must allow the knife

---

* blade A. leaf OE.; spathe of grass xiv. B. broad flattened part of an implement OE.; thin cutting edge, sword xiv. OE. blæd, pl. bladu = OS. blad, OHG. blat (G. blatt), ON. blað leaf, etc. :- Gmc. *blaðam, perh. pp. formation (IE. *-tos) on the base *blð- BLOW. The present form derives from OE.obl. cases. (Source: *The Concise Oxford Dictionary of English Etymology*, OUP 1986.)

to roll. It doesn't matter whether it's made of German tool steel or from a hacksaw blade and recycled pallet wood.

It is intriguing how many cultures have taken a single 'master' knife and developed it to serve many purposes – the chef's knife and the *cai dao* spring first to mind – yet also how another tradition, like the Japanese, has seen such value in the idea that they've absorbed it into their own knifemaking with developments like the *santoku*. Watching how the cultures now cross-fertilise – how Western chefs revere Japanese blades, how every chef's knife roll, in every culture, now contains a *santoku* as well as a chef's knife, how the Japanese have responded by adopting and improving double grinding, and how chef's knives are evolving wider and lighter blades – is equally fascinating.

It's tantalising to imagine that all this evolution might one day result in a couple of designs of hybrid 'Überknife'. Imagine a blade as sharp as a *yanagiba* with a deep blade echoing the *cai dao*, the chef's knife and the *usuba*, a handle combining the heft and grip of the Western style with the easy rolling action of the *wa* style, a bolster to protect the finger, the versatility of the *santoku*, as easy for machines to replicate as a German blade, as seemly and light as a Japanese one. Sure, it might break with a thousand traditions, but as a symbol of what cooks and knifemakers across the world and throughout human history have evolved together, it would be a wonderful thing to add to your roll.

A kitchen knife carries a cultural, historical and technological load out of all proportion to its simple structure. A knife has a beautiful purity of purpose, it's almost the perfect expression of form that precisely follows function, and yet it is at once a seething mess of elusive, impalpable qualities. To pick up a knife, to feel its heft and weight, is to connect with all of this. There are cultures that would speak of the 'spirit' of the blade, but I'm a little too British for that; instead, this book is an essay of praise for the knife, an exploration of its material self but, more, a celebration of its intangibles.

ANATOMY OF THE KNIFE

···

THE TWO MAIN STRUCTURES of the knife are the *blade* and *handle* but there's a much more complicated nomenclature for its various parts.

The blade has a *point*, a *spine** and, if it curves along the bottom, a *belly*. When describing the position on the blade we refer to the *heel*, near the handle, and the *tip*, towards the point.

The *bevel* describes the way the blade is ground more thinly from the spine to the cutting edge and the *face* or *cheek* is the flat ground† surface.

The metal of the blade continues into the handle for strength and stability, in a portion called the *tang*. In Japanese blades, traditionally used with light strokes, the tang is a forged spike that's stuck into a solid wooden handle. In most Western-pattern knives and those used for a more percussive style of chopping, the tang forms a central layer right through the handle – a *full tang*. In these cases the handle is formed of two plates or *scales* sandwiched either side of the tang and held together with *rivets*. The end of the handle is called the *butt* and in some knives may be a knob-like metal extension of the tang.

In some blades, particularly German-made chef's knives, a swelling is forged into the metal where blade meets handle. This is the *bolster*, which serves to strengthen the blade, to make it more intuitive so that the proper professional applies a 'pinch' grip, and to protect the fingers. This is the modern equivalent of the wonderfully named *ricasso*. The *ricasso* is the short, unsharpened portion of the blade just before it reaches the handle in early duelling weapons, where the forefinger could be wrapped over the handguard and laid against the blade for better grip. Where the blade joins a wood handle there is usually a *ferrule* made of bone or horn to stop the wood splitting.

---

* As if it wasn't weird enough that we imbue knives with character and spirit, most of the parts of the knife are named after parts of our bodies.

† A double-ground blade, common in the West, is sharpened equally on both sides, giving a symmetrical wedge shape. A single-ground blade is sharpened on one side only, giving a more acute angle.

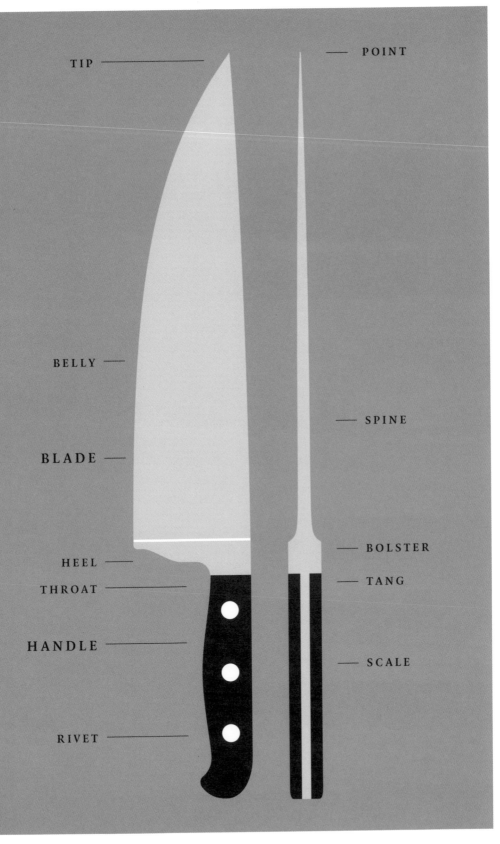

TIP

POINT

BELLY

SPINE

BLADE

BOLSTER

HEEL

TANG

THROAT

HANDLE

SCALE

RIVET

ON GRIP

....

THE WAY YOUR HAND FITS A KNIFE is an infinitely variable combination of hand size, handle shape, intention in cutting and culinary tradition. Nevertheless, there are five basic grip styles.

1. **HAMMER GRIP.** This is the way most people hold a cleaver or chopper: a strong, firm grasp with all the fingers wrapped around the handle one way and the thumb in opposition. It's the natural grip for a striking blow but means that all control of the angle of the blade is through the wrist. It feels strong but not finely controllable. If you use a hatchet or axe frequently you'll remember how much practice it took to get consecutive blows to land in the same place. Try cutting something big and tough, like a cabbage, with a less than sharp knife, however, and you'll automatically assume the hammer grip – there's no other way through.

2. **PINCH GRIP.** A fencer is taught to hold the foil between the tips of the thumb and forefinger, just under the guard. This creates a pivot through many degrees of freedom and the whole blade can be moved against it with the remaining three fingers. The chef's pinch grip works on a similar principle. The thumb and forefinger grip the back of the blade where the spine joins the handle, just in front of the bolster, and the remaining fingers fall loosely along the rest of the handle. The blade, pivoting on its point, can be moved rapidly up and down to fine-chop but the tip can be controlled, like the fencer's foil, with the rest of the hand. This grip feels delicate and massively controlled but, as it's poor at transmitting brute force, it relies on a wicked cutting edge.

3. **POINT GRIP.** It's a weird quirk of human physiology and psychology that we become amazingly accurate at calculating, at an unconscious and instinctive level, exactly where our forefinger is pointing. You don't need to squint along your finger, like sighting a gun, in order to know that it's pointing at something. It's one of those mind/muscle things, like catching a ball, for which we're somehow

deep-programmed.[*] Placing the forefinger along the spine of the knife 'locks' the blade into that instinct – an extension of the arm. Control over direction is total, though ability to exert serious pressure, except in a direct, thrusting action, is much reduced. A blade held this way needs to be sharp enough to cut easily in long, sweeping strokes. This is how sashimi chefs use their *yanagibas*.[†]

4. **DAGGER GRIP.** Similar to the hammer grip but with the blade tip facing in the opposite direction, out of the bottom of your hand. This grip is only really used by commercial butchers, hunters or fishermen, where the carcass is hanging or laid out on a bench. Holding the knife like this means you can exert enormous strength and the natural swing of the blade is away from your other hand. If you're cutting down sides of beef or tuna all day, that's a reassuring safety feature.

5. **TOWARD-THE-THUMB GRIP.** This takes a narrow blade and a small handle because the knife must be fully held and controlled by the four fingers wrapped around it. The cutting edge faces the thumb, which is used to push material on to it. This is the grip used to sharpen a pencil or whittle a point on a piece of wood and is the only time it's ever permissible to cut towards a part of your body. The main skill is to cut fast and accurately without hitting the fleshy part of the thumb, which is why the curved French *tourné* knife in particular has such a complex geometry.

---

[*] 'Everyone has the ability to point at an object. When a soldier points, he instinctively points at the feature on the object on which his eyes are focused. An impulse from the brain causes the arm and hand to stop when the finger reaches the proper position. When the eyes are shifted to a new object or feature, the finger, hand, and arm also shift to this point. It is this inherent trait that can be used by a soldier to rapidly and accurately engage targets.'
US Army Field Manual 3–23.35: Combat Training With Pistols M9 AND M11 (June, 2003).

[†] Surgeons are trained to use the 'point' grip on the scalpel for long initial incisions then to shift to the 'pinch' grip for dissection. The two raised circles on either side of a standard scalpel handle show where the pinch is made.

KNIFE STROKES

IN ORDER TO CUT, the blade must be moved through the material. The motion of the blade while cutting falls into seven styles, six of which require the second hand to adopt 'The Claw' (see opposite).

1. **CHOP.** The whole blade moves up and down vertically, remaining parallel to the cutting surface.

2. **ROCKING CHOP.** The rounded tip of the blade remains in contact with the board while it pivots down. This most useful action can be used lightly, when mincing herbs for example, or as a way of maintaining safe control on a really tough cut – when cutting through a big chicken joint, for example, it's usual to rock back to locate the joint then hold down the tip with one hand and transfer full weight above the handle to push safely down and through the cartilage.

3. **PUSH SLICE.** Slide the blade forward, parallel to the cutting board, allowing the weight of the knife – or very light hand pressure – to carry it down until blade touches board. This is the classic Western vegetable slicing motion.

4. **PULL SLICE.** Engage the heel of the blade and pull back and down in a single stroke – the sashimi cut. It's similar in every sense to the push slice although sashimi chefs reputedly don't allow the blade edge to touch the cutting board at the end of the cut.

5. **'LOCOMOTIVE'.** For fast vegetable work the blade is pushed forwards and halfway through and then pulled back and down, touching the board and then coming up again – a kind of circular chopping/slicing action with the forearm working like a piston on a train.

6. **SAWING CUT.** If you're holding a serrated bread knife and slicing some stale bread, a sawing motion is OK. If you're sawing with any other kind of knife, it's blunt and you need to stop and sharpen it.

These are all descriptions of vertical cuts but all can be achieved at various angles to the board.

7. **HORIZONTAL CUT.** Horizontal cuts are not common in Western cooking and they're the only ones where the claw is not used. When brunoising onions, a couple of partial horizontal cuts are necessary and these are achieved – with extraordinary care – while pushing the onion half to the board with the fingertips, keeping the rest of the hand high and away in case the knife slips. The other main horizontal cut is the utterly lethal and desperate 'last slice' cut, in which a piece of (usually) bread or meat is squashed flat to the board with the palm of the hand, the fingers stretched back and up in fervent but usually futile hope, and the blade sawn between hand and board.

I realise that there are occasions in even the best kitchens when the last piece has to be stretched to two portions, but for me, this particular cut has too many options for horrific slips. The *cai dao* is used with a raised chopping block that gives knuckle clearance when the blade is used horizontally. As a result horizontal cutting is safer, easier and much more common in Chinese kitchens (see page 76).

THE CLAW

....

It would be natural to assume that the knife is a 'one-handed' tool but in reality all cutting involves the other hand, offering material up to the blade and stabilising it during the cut. As important as the grasp on the knife itself is 'The Claw' – using the tips of the fingers and the backs of the fingernails to hold the food steady and creating a flat vertical surface with the 'middle phalanx'* along which the flat of the knife can slide. The tips of the fingers are rolled back towards the palm meaning that, in normal use, the knife cannot possibly cut them.

The claw means you can make an extremely rapid chopping action while gently sliding the food past the knife with your fingernail – the wonderful flashy trick of onion chopping so beloved of TV chefs.

Practise the claw whenever you can because without this strange gesture of your spare hand, even the best knives in the world are useless.

---

* Working backwards from the tip, your finger has three phalanges – distal, middle and proximal.

ON MATERIALS

....

IN ITS MOST BASIC FORM, knifemaking began with naturally occurring rocks. Flint, found in areas of sedimentary rock, and obsidian are brittle rocks that, because of their molecular structure, break with a characteristic conchoidal or 'shell-shaped' fracture pattern.* Bash a couple of pieces together and you'll notice how the cracked edges conspire to create a lethally sharp, naturally serrated blade, easily sharp enough to cut raw meat or to carve bone and wood. As the earliest humans developed flint-knapping techniques, various cultures created stone knives of increasingly refined shape and delicacy, but the cutting edge was the result of the original, natural fractures. The edge could never be improved by polishing or grinding, at least not with Stone Age methods, and, though the elegant, highly wrought knife of a chieftain might look impressive when tucked into his antelope-skin belt, it would never be substantially better at doing its job than a freshly cracked rock. Yet the fact that the earliest toolmakers were already creating knives in which beauty was, to some degree, more important than pure function must imply that they were already beginning to imbue them with more abstract values.

Copper and bronze knives appeared as man discovered how to work with these new materials, but these earliest metals were easy to extract and refine because of their softness. A soft metal can make a light arrowhead or a serviceable stabbing weapon but is worse than hopeless at holding a working cutting edge. Even once bronze was created, the best thing for cutting up meat may still have been a flint knife. With the arrival of iron, though, we start to see edged knives with real potential.

Extracting iron from ore, a process known as smelting, involves heating it, melting it and driving off impurities. This is the basic process that begins with rock and ends with rough metal, but it is only the beginning of a series of actions that can alter the qualities of metal in innumerable ways. Smelted iron – sometimes called 'pig iron' – is hard, can be cast into shapes and can be strong but it's extremely brittle. You could cast a knife in iron but if you dropped it on a hard surface, it would probably break. Steel, on the other hand, an alloy of pure iron with up to 2 per cent carbon, is strong and flexible. It is both *malleable*, meaning it can be pressed into shape without shattering, and *ductile*, meaning it can be stretched into shape without snapping. The

---

* The pattern is caused by the shockwave which moves from the point of impact like ripples on a pond. As cracking in rocks caused by temperature change occurs in flat planes, the presence of conchoidal fracture patterns in rocks is often accepted as an indicator of human intervention.

qualities that matter most in a knife are its resistance to snapping, the ability to take an edge, how long the edge lasts, and how easy it is to resharpen. Perhaps less vital to function but no less important to the owner will be resistance to corrosion and aesthetic beauty.

By varying the amount of carbon it's possible to create steels along continua of hardness, flexibility and workability. Alloying it with small percentages of other metals can also alter its colour and durability.

Iron and steel can be *cast*, that is, poured when molten into a mould and allowed to harden, or they can be *forged*, which means that a piece is heated until soft and then forced into shape, either by pressure or beating. The rough piece out of which a blade is made could be moulded from molten metal, beaten out of hot lump with hammers, squeezed flat between vast rollers, stretched like noodles or even extruded, like white-hot toothpaste, through a shaped hole. Each of these techniques alters some of the qualities of the original material, as do various heat treatments. Steel, in fact, though a metaphor for permanence, solidity and purity, is, within its parameters, an infinitely variable substance.

Look at a machine-made knife, perhaps a Wüsthof Dreizack Classic 4584/26 like the one on page 52. A blank of steel, an alloy containing exact ratios of chromium (Cr), molybenum (Mo) and vanadium (V) with a laboratory-tested Rockwell Hardness of 56, has been carefully selected for its material virtues. It has been forged by giant machines exerting unimaginable force, ground by computer-guided mills precise to the micron in their choreography. The heat treatment will have been controlled to a hundredth of a degree and the finished blade tested to unimaginably high standards. If, like me, you get excited by tech, then this is one of those objects that represents the pinnacle of what human science, design and technology can achieve. To hold it in your hand is to grasp all of that. Like a replacement human joint or an engine component in a million-dollar jet fighter, every single knife coming off the line will be identical – and these are some of the most gorgeous knives in the world, utterly efficient and surgically fit for purpose.

Now consider a knife made in another tradition. A hard steel for a sharp edge is wrapped like a sandwich in a softer, less brittle steel. For an hour or so it's hammered flat by a man who's guided by no more complex computer than the one in his own skull. His 'pattern' is experience. The temperature control for heat treatment is his judgement of the colour that the metal glows. He will beat the hot sandwich of metal until molecular change is wrought between the layers. Carbon from his furnace will combine with the metal surface and the crystalline structure of the metals will, in places, be realigned by the blows of his hammer. This knife will never see a lab, no one could call its material anything as homogenising as 'CroMoV', and the final

HEAT TREATMENT

....

Traditionally, heat-treating metal meant placing it in a forge until the temperature, judged by colour, was correct, then 'quenching' it in water or oil. This rough process conveniently serves to harden steel or cast iron. What is actually happening is that the microcrystalline structure of the metal is being altered and it can be done with much more refinement. Holding metal at certain high heats over varying periods of time or precisely controlling cooling can alter the qualities of the metal in much more subtle ways.

I visited a modern heat-treatment plant to watch some knife blanks being treated. It was a low-rise workshop on an industrial estate outside Derby, nondescript and anonymous from the outside but – with dripping, crusted pots of molten cyanide salt in rows, chains dangling from the ceiling on blood-chilling hooks and a constant throbbing roar like the mouth of a jet engine – a circle of medieval Hades within. It wasn't, however, served by sweating demons or kobolds stripped to their loincloths, but by a nice chap called Simon. Here, he explained, they can make almost any metal do almost anything. By heating to many thousands of degrees in those pots of molten salt, they can control the chemical content and molecular structure of components to incredible tolerances.

'What d'you reckon that is?' he asked, throwing me a dull, matte grey metal mushroom with an inexplicable and disturbing weight to it... 'Once that's got the thread turned into it, it'll be the bolt that holds down the lid on a transport vessel for nuclear waste.'

Our bunch of blanks was heated gently up to around 500°c in an empty pot. 'Just a warm bath to get them used to the idea,' said Simon, before they were lowered into a molten salt bath at around 1200°c for 10 minutes. Tiny motes flickered spontaneously on the surface as we watched. It was absurdly pretty but the temperature was like nothing I've ever experienced, a manifestation of heat that made the air feel too solid to breathe. Simon lifted the blades clear of the salt bath, danced them across the workshop floor like live fish on a rod and lowered them carefully into a vast tank of sinister black oil which seethed malevolently as they cooled.

This is not, perhaps, the way small craftsman knifemakers have worked in the past but they are beginning to experiment. Imagine a big chef's knife that can bend centimetres off-centre and spring straight back. Imagine an entirely rigid blade that doesn't need a thick, heavy spine. The possibilities are thrilling.

measure of its hardness will be not Rockwell, but the cook who takes it home. If you are excited by craftsmanship then this is one of those objects that represents a whole civilisation's evolution of creativity and ingenuity, and the expression of an individual artist's skill. These are some of the most beautiful knives in the world, no two alike at any level, challenging to use, a chore to maintain and breathtakingly beautiful.

There is currently a huge resurgence of craft knifemaking across the world – not just, as one might expect, in Japan. Craftsmen like Bob Kramer in the States (see page 61) or Joel Black in the UK, collectives like Doghouse or Blenheim Forge are turning out amazing blades bursting with character, buzzing with spirit.

In use, it's hard to choose between the awe-inspiring technology and precision that go into an engineered knife and the craftsmanship that goes into a hand-built one, but I wanted to find out more about the process. I needed to make a knife.

ON MAKING A KNIFE

....

THE BLADE BEGINS with a drift of steel pieces, like thick foil. You can cut them to shape with a straightedge and a Stanley knife. We count them and then carefully stack them on to the end of a steel bar. With a few swift passes of a small welding torch they're roughly stitched together, like a mille-feuille pastry on the end of a stick.

Outside the workshop, ranged along a scarred bench, is the forge, made from an old propane cylinder, on its side and raised on metal legs. The top has been cut out and the inside lined with a thick blanket of mineral wool. A gas pipe, attached to a regulator and shoved through a hole in the side of the cylinder, wakes with a woof and within minutes the forge is glowing – a roaring maw, pulsing between orange and white through a disorientating heat haze. I shove the laminated metal stack into the forge and maneuver it close to the flame. Soon it too is glowing, so I withdraw it and sprinkle the glowing tip with borax, then thrust it back into the heat.* The borax melts and bubbles and, after a few more dustings, we lift the glowing lump into the forging press.

At its heart, the forging press is a hydraulic ram, the kind of thing you'll see lifting the back of a dump truck or the arm of a digger. Around this is welded a frame of square-section steel girders so the entire pressure of the ram is applied to closing two steel blocks together in an area about the size of a bar of chocolate.

A hydraulic ram this size might easily lift a large car on to a truck. Imagine that pressure applied against an immovable surface. Imagine your fingers trapped in there... no, maybe not. But the pressure is certainly enough to begin squashing the glowing hot metal plates together. Each actuation of the ram crushes the metal sheets tighter and tighter together until they begin to unify. Maybe twenty times we lift the metal from the forge to the press, sprinkle it with borax and crush it again with the whole power of the ram.

Now the metal sandwich is a homogenous piece and the hand-forging can begin. We hold the metal in the flame until it's glowing madly, then lift it out on to the anvil and clobber it with a short sledgehammer.

---

* Borax (Sodium tetraborate) is a salt of boric acid and is used as a flux. It lowers the melting point of iron oxide, which allows it to burn off. Unrefined borax is sometimes called tincar, which may give us the word 'tinker' for an itinerant tinsmith. Borax is also used as a food-preserving salt and may have been the 'natron' used to preserve some of the bodies of the pharaohs.

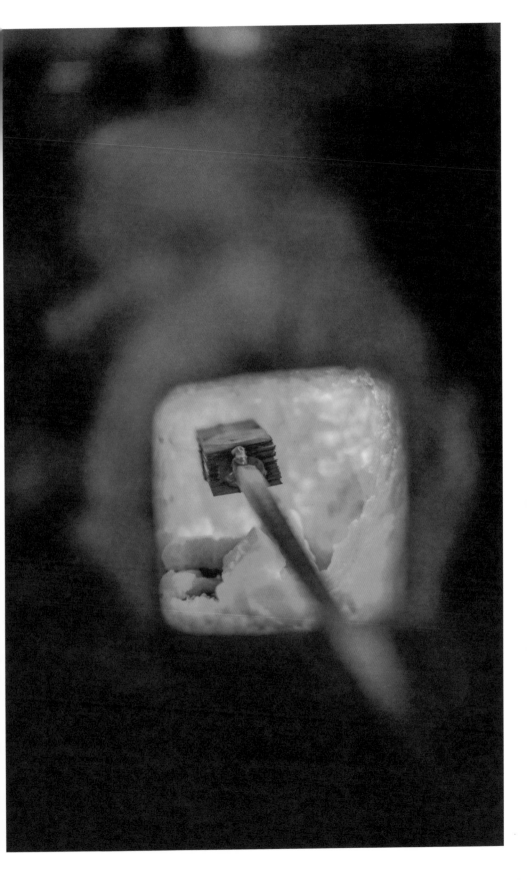

I had thought, before today, of red-hot metal as flexible, perhaps the consistency of hard Plasticine, but, in reality it's still hard. Heat, at this level, only softens the metal a little. Essentially, you're wailing away at something only marginally softer than the solid, cold metal of the anvil, but with the added frisson of terror that, at this temperature, it could burn through clothing and flesh in micro-seconds. The upside to this is that it's hard to go wrong: no single blow with the hammer is sufficient to truly mess up your blade. On the other hand, repeating the same blow again and again is beyond exhausting.

I'm not a small man; in fact, I'm probably built bigger than the knifemaker, but after 20 or so blows I can hardly swing the hammer; my forearm begins to cramp and my shoulders scream. The professional steps in and shows me how to let the hammer fall – just guiding it gently, letting it bounce and only putting in the smallest effort at the very top of the swing.

With this technique it's possible to keep hammering for much longer; I reckon it takes around 200 blows between us before the blade is roughly in shape.

Now we quench the hot blade in oil, a process that hardens the knife a little, then we draw on to it with a Sharpie, tracing the shape of the blade from a cardboard template. Using a huge pair of bench mounted shears with a long handle for leverage, we nip away spare shards of the beaten blade to create the correct 'profile'. Now it is time to take it to the wheel.

The wheel is about a metre and a half in diameter and 15 centimetres (6 inches) thick, mounted in a wooden frame, half boxed in and equipped with a powerful electric motor at its axle. The motor starts and over five minutes, it slowly comes up to speed. The wheel weighs only a little less than I do and it's now spinning at 7,000 rpm. When the power is switched off it will take nearly 15 minutes to slow to a halt. If it were to break loose from its bearings it would crash through the brick wall it faces (and possibly the two neighbouring houses). I must lie along the casing and over the wheel.

A water spray cools the surface and keeps down the dust but it still feels terrifying to be lying face down on something so powerful and applying steel to its surface just inches from your face. Slowly, in showers of water, steam and spark, the blade begins to take shape. Again the process is slow. The metal is abraded slowly so it's easy not to push things too far.

There is more to be done to the blade by hands much more skilled than mine but it now looks the part. It's an ugly thing – dark, matt, rough-surfaced and crude but there's something else, something much more powerful. In a few hours I have watched thousands of joules of energy pour into this lump of metal. Thousands of degrees of heat, tons of hydraulically applied pressure and the hundreds of hammer blows that had completely exhausted my upper body. Of course, I know enough physics to explain exactly how the energy was disseminated and yet, the feeling of it remains in the blade. It feels like if I could find the right switch, all that power might stream back out, like some kind of culinary light-saber.

It's a strange revelation. Sure, machines are used to make your car engine or watch, but that happens in a controlled, distant way in a factory. Hand-forging a knife is a process just primitive enough to make the effort involved explicit, and in a strange way, it somehow manages to contain and store that.

A popular fashion among knife aficionados at the moment is Damascus steel, forged from blocks made up from many layers of metal to create a gorgeous, textured effect when polished and etched. I'm a rigorous advocate of form following function, so I used to wonder why we bother with Damascus finish on knife blades. Laminating had some purpose in swords – it was important that your blade was strong enough to strike another without shattering – but when your opponent is a tomato, Damascus is just an affectation. But now I see it differently. A Damascus blade shows the world what was done to it in its making. The effort that went into beating 65 pieces of steel together to make this blade is manifest – and the display is beautiful.

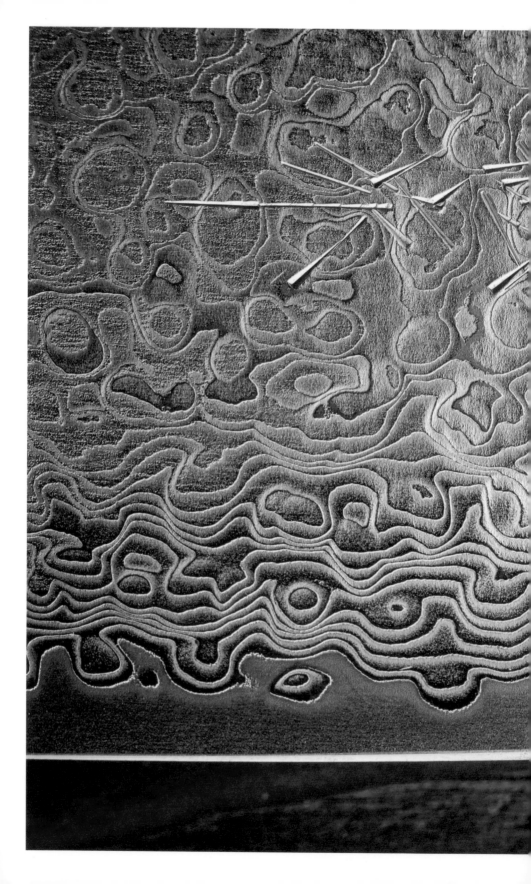

ON KNIFEMAKERS

....

JONATHAN WARSHAWSKY, James Ross-Harris and Richard Warner are, collectively, Blenheim Forge, among the very few British knifemakers who both specialise in culinary blades and forge their own metal.* There is something, perhaps, in spending long days, repeatedly beating the hell out of red-hot metal, that warps your perception of time, but knifemakers seem to work to a different clock to the rest of the world. There was a considerable wait before our meeting could begin. Jon lopes in first. He's covered in the film that varnishes anyone who works with grinders – a mix of oil, dirt, metal dust and rust.

I ask how they'd started knifemaking...

JW: James and I were living in the same house and we had some free time on our hands. We got into doing these DIY projects, I guess you would call them, over the weekends, just to pass the time. We tried to build a welder out of a microwave; we made a meat smoker, a barbecue; we had this hot-tub jacuzzi thing going in the garden. I was doing my PhD in philosophy and I spent many hours just over a computer or book. If you spend too long staring at the screen you kind of get this itch in your fingers. So, I guess I needed some sort of relief from that constant thinking.

Between our projects, we would look at a lot of stuff on the Internet, on YouTube. If, last week, you tried to make a barbecue and a welder, YouTube will automatically recommend for you, 'How about this video? How about a knife?' I'm not necessarily proud of it, but yes, that's the way it happened. We didn't set out with an idea in mind. We watched the video and we thought this might be an interesting project.

I was also working as a carpenter at the time, doing furniture recycling – 'upcycling', they called it – and JRH was working as a welder. We were working in jobs where you need a lot of expensive tools and machinery and where there's little hope of setting up on your own. But knifemaking felt like all you needed was an anvil and a hammer and fire and you're good to go, or so we thought. So, one Sunday we got a load of old files from Peckham market and some scrap bits of steel, laid them out, and tried to make a Damascus billet.

---

* ...rather than buying pre-forged 'blanks' from specialist suppliers.

To anyone who's spent time around knifemakers, this is an almost laughably naïve idea. Most will cheerfully talk for hours about how long they took beating scrap into rough, failed blades before they ever dreamed they could tackle the complexities of Damascus, but this seemed to have escaped the Blenheim Boys...

We hadn't done nearly enough research and had no idea about the intricacies. We didn't know anything about anything. We used the wrong methods, the wrong temperatures, but it worked out, for some reason, doing all the wrong things and we had a finished knife. It shouldn't have happened, really. And that gave us motivation. Because it was so easy to do that, we thought, 'Oh, let's make a whole set of them', and started thinking of different sizes. Then we spent over a year trying to reproduce that initial success, because we made the forge at home, and we got a tiny anvil, and we just couldn't do it. We'd say, 'Okay, we'll try a different temperature', and it was just the first billet that welded that gave us this feeling, 'Oh, this is really easy to do.'

It was an amazing stroke of luck. There was every chance, if that first experiment had failed, that they'd have moved on to brewing or spoon carving, but knifemaking had got under their skins...

We might never have tried again, or, maybe twice, three times more and said, 'No, this is way too complicated', and gone on to the next thing. But, when you succeed the first time, you know you can do it; it's that easy. That insane belief that you could spend an hour and you've got a knife fuelled a whole year of frustrations. It took us into a pretty dark place in the end. We'd prep a billet, go to work, come back, not even change clothes, go on out to the garden, light the forge and try and weld it. That would fail. You'd go to sleep, having nightmares about steel and fire just destroying itself. All the intensity of your studying transposed completely into thumping metal.

James and Richard enter the café oblivious to the consternation of the neatly groomed clientele. They've been shifting a huge power hammer to their new workshop and, frankly, they make Jon look clean.

JRH: It was quite successful, actually. Could've been way worse.

RW: Easy enough.

JW: I quit carpentry pretty early on, but it was a while before we moved into the workshop, and a while from there before it became... before we sold anything. I think we started off giving away knives as gifts, and yes, it was a long time before we felt we had a product that was okay to sell to someone. They were gifts for a long time, and his cousins got one, my Mum.

JRH: Yes, and then we kind of started selling them on the understanding that if they went wrong, we would replace them, basically, to locals. I mean, you can't just start making good knives straight away. You can't suddenly produce great knives, having made one or two. You need a lot of practice at making them, and our lives are a lot better now, and we make them a lot faster, so it's viable, but previously, the amount of hours that went into each knife was a lot longer, and there's some massive learning curves as well.

RW: It's partly the tools, to start with. If we'd had 20 grand to spend on tools on day one, then it would've happened a lot quicker.

JRH: But it wouldn't have been the best way of doing it. I think the process we took, we probably learnt a lot more. We wouldn't have known what the right tools were, for starters.

JW: Looking back, we could have cut a lot of that time just going and learning it professionally with someone, but we had this whole process of experimentation learning to do it ourselves. That meant being able to recognise many of the mistakes that you can make. We also had a certain privilege that none of us really needed this to succeed really fast, or we were not... I mean, we've got reasonable rent where we live, things like that...

JRH: Yes, it didn't matter, really. The workshop rent's quite cheap and for the first year the sales we made paid the bills and what was left over just went into tools. We still had our part-time jobs so it was like it didn't matter. Before I went full-time I was doing three days a week welding. I kind of just ran out of money when we started making money. That means starting to pay yourself, rather than buying more tools.

JW: ...organic growth, I guess.

There are enough dreadlocks in the room that I feel able to ask the uncomfortably New Age question: does a knife have anything like a spirit?

JRH: I'd say they're all different. It starts from the beginning, every hammer strike is in a slightly different place, and then when you're grinding it, you're looking at where the core is, and if the hammering's different, then you have to adjust for that. At the very beginning of the process, when you're squashing the steel in the press, that is essentially affecting how it's going to look at the end. So, those initial strikes and squashes determine everything. We've changed our process quite a lot, experimenting with different things, and the results are definitely different. It's a lot of learning, but I think we're at the stage where our knives are coming out consistently good.

So is a particular style developing from their work together?

JRH: I think we've always had a kind of vague idea of what we wanted our knives to be like. No fancy handles, just quite simple, focussing on the blade rather than anything else.

They're Japanese-style, but we wouldn't pretend to call ourselves 'Japanese knife-makers'. I think Damascus techniques existed all over the world,* I don't know why this has happened, but in more recent history it's become associated with Japan.

JW: The shapes of the blades and the angles of the sharpening, the handles, those things are, I guess, Japanese-influenced.

JRH: Well, and the steel types, as well.

JW: The steel, yes, the hardness of the steel, things like that are Japanese-influenced, or inspired.

At the moment, there's a queue, months long, for a Blenheim Forge knife. Celebrities are having them custom-made. The media have caught on to the ruffian charm of these three photogenically grubby young men making beautiful objects. I wonder what the plan is... TV... retail... licensing deals... What's the Exit Strategy?

JW: More knives.

JRH: Keep going, I think. Keep going. Anyone got any other plans?

JW: No.

RW: Not really.

JRH: I think we'll stick with kitchen knives for a good while; that's kind of our thing, I suppose.

RW: ...just, sort of, building up a reputation and maintaining it.

JRH: I think so, yes. We're still learning a lot. We're definitely still improving. Daily, weekly, we're improving.

---

* The name 'Damascus' has complicated and curious roots. It was originally a pattern in metalwork from Damascus in Syria which had been forged from a steel called 'Wootz' imported from India. The steel was refined by an arcane process, now long lost, which involved sealing iron ore in clay crucibles and firing them at high temperatures. The resulting ingots were full of impurities and composed of iron and various steel alloys, but these formed in layers which both strengthened the metal and gave it beautiful markings. Modern Damascus steel attempts to mimic the original Wootz by layering carefully selected steel alloys and crushing them together under great heat and pressure until they form a similar 'wafer' structure, a process more accurately called 'Pattern Welding'. The assembled billets of metal can be twisted, cut, punched, folded or otherwise distressed during forging to create a variety of patterns. Metallurgists constantly try to emulate Wootz without much success so, until they get it right, we'll have to content ourselves with our own, beautiful 'Damascus'.

BLENHEIM
FORGE

TOP LEFT: JON WARSHAWSKY
TOP RIGHT: JAMES ROSS-HARRIS
BOTTOM LEFT: RICHARD WARNER

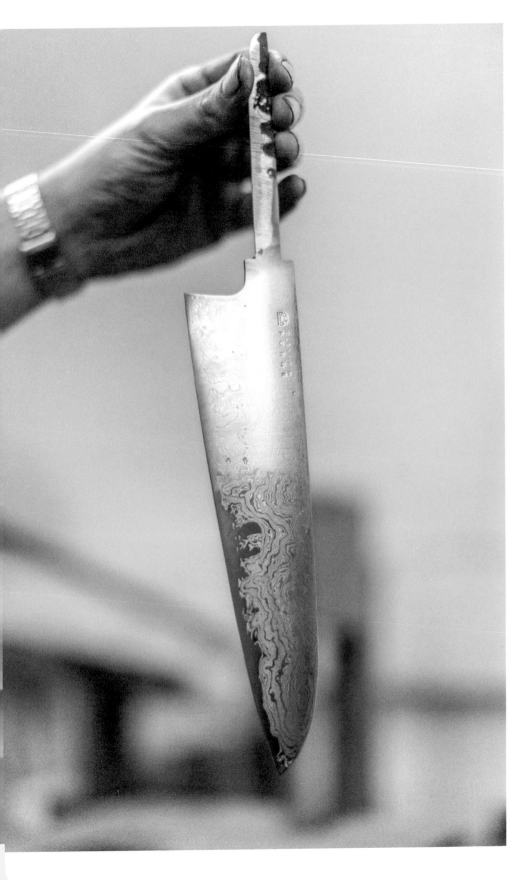

THE KNIVES

ON THE COOK'S KNIVES

....

IN A ROLL, A TOOLBOX, on a rack or stuffed in a drawer, your set of knives is more than the sum of its parts. They might have been inherited or quietly nicked from other cooks, complicated and expensive purchases may have been made, but however you come by your knives, your kit is in an active process of evolution. A useless knife is got rid of, a damaged one either rejected or coaxed back into productive life. You might sharpen them obsessively or feel a constant, nagging, low-grade guilt that you 'really ought to get round to' a spot of maintenance. As your skills develop, you'll outgrow old favourites, aspire to new ones and eventually acquire them. No wonder people get obsessed about their roll… it's a chillingly accurate snapshot of their character.

There always seems to be a master knife in the kit, the one that's in your hand the most. The classic chef's knife, based on the time-honoured French pattern, is the master knife in our culinary tradition. This makes sense because most high-quality Western cooking – at least as far as it's formally trained – is based on French. A modern chef could pick up Escoffier's knife and use it easily, and he would, had he got his hands on one, have been very comfortable with the contemporary version.

The curved blade rocks to mince meat and herbs, the length enables slices to be cut from big slabs of protein, the handle sits high so knuckles clear the cutting board. Chefs pride themselves on being able to do almost anything they need in the kitchen with just the one knife. It's perhaps unsurprising that buying a chef's knife is the first thing one does on self-defining as a serious cook. Sure, your mum had knives, you probably used one or two in grubby kitchens as a student, but the day you go out and intentionally drop £50 or more on a knife is the day you declare to the world that you're not just someone who makes dinner, you're now a cook.

Elizabeth David is often credited with relaunching serious cooking in the UK after the war and she saw the knife as key to taking cooking seriously. Though stainless-steel kitchen knives were available, she preferred the French provincial favourite, carbon steel – softer and easier to sharpen. Many older cooks still have a soft spot for the Davidian Sabatier with which they discovered garlic, olives and lemons – conveniently forgetting that the blade rusted like a bugger and turned the lemons black – and very few have survived the intervening sixty years of enthusiastic sharpening.

Today, the professional chef's knife is more likely to have been made in Germany than in France, with Wüsthof and Henckels the two main competitors in the field. They are so beautifully, so scientifically manufactured that notions of individual 'craftsmanship' seem strangely distant. Their efficiency is total, their finish so flawless

PLEASE FIND ENCLOSED YOUR PERSONALLY
SIGNED COPY OF

KN FE

TIM HAYWARD

THE CULTURE, CRAFT

AND CULT OF THE

COOK'S KNIFE

IF YOU WOULD LIKE TO SHOW YOUR SUPPORT,
PLEASE TWEET/INSTAGRAM:

@TIMHAYWARD @QUADRILLEFOOD @QUADRILLEBOOKS
#KNIFEBOOK

THANK YOU!

that it seems impossible to imagine that a human was involved in their creation and that is, in a strange way, reassuring. Like some gleaming component of an aircraft I'm flying in, I kind of don't want to believe that these knives were beaten into shape by a bloke with a hammer.

The secondary knives in the rack are the ones that do things the big knife can't. Boning and filleting require thinner, more flexible blades and often there will be a knife designed for an altogether different type of cutting – the kind of 'toward-the-thumb' whittling that works so well on vegetables. There's no way the 8-inch knife can be wielded that way: the deep throat that enables the knuckles to clear the chopping board puts the cutting edge in quite the wrong place.

The standard roll for a culinary student today will probably include the chef's knife, a boner, a flexible filleter, a paring knife and a turning knife.

Beyond this most cooks accumulate 'special' knives. Weird one-off specials that do one thing too well to ignore. Old-school classically trained pros will have a couple of melon ballers. These spoon-shaped cutters were routinely stolen from the pastry chef because they were so fast at coring tomatoes and cucumbers. I know one chef who keeps her grandfather's pocket knife just for removing the eyes from potatoes. I'm a great fan of the devilled kidney so I keep a small pair of locking forceps and a 10a scalpel for efficiently whipping out the fibrous cores.

The last thing in the kit will be an old favourite. A knife that's lived its life too well and too long and should really, by rights, have been retired years ago. But it's hard... really hard... to say goodbye to a tool you've loved and used. A tool you've adapted to use, whose shape you've formed. One that's given blameless and brilliant service.

There will always be that single old stager because, though all tools are about efficiency, function and fitness for purpose, knives have an extra emotional dimension. It's the part that demands that we care for our knives and it's the part that gives us a kind of 'pride in the roll'.

FRENCH KNIVES

CHEF'S KNIFE

UTILITY

PARING

TOURNÉ

FILLETING

CLEAVER

BUTCHER

JAPANESE KNIVES

HANKOTSU

PETTY

SANTOKU

GYUTO

USUBA

DEBA

YANAGIBA

WESTERN KNIVES

CHEF'S KNIFE

....

BLADE LENGTH: **200MM/260MM**
OVERALL LENGTH: **330MM/450MM**
WEIGHT: **222G/340G**
MANUFACTURED BY: **WÜSTHOF**
MATERIALS: **FORGED CROMOV STEEL WITH A ROCKWELL HARDNESS OF 56, POLYMER**
COUNTRY OF ORIGIN: **GERMANY**
USES: **GENERAL PURPOSE**

....

THE WÜSTHOF DREIZACK CLASSIC 4584 RANGE are possibly the most desirable of all French-pattern kitchen knives. They're wider than standard, making the knife heavier and giving just over an extra centimetre of clearance at the throat – good if you have big hands. Like most German manufacturers, Wüsthof favour a bolster design which makes a proper 'pinch' grip on the back of the blade more comfortable over a long day's work.

The 8-inch is a gorgeously balanced knife and makes chopping a pleasure, but in skilled hands even the 10-inch – a monstrous great culinary 'Excalibur' – is as truly multi-purpose a tool as a *cai dao*. In a single shift a professional will use it for everything from chiffonading herbs, through boning a chicken and then back to brunoising carrots at high speed. The back ('spine') of the blade is used to crush herbs, the side to smash garlic to a pulp and the tip sharp enough for delicate surgical tasks like whipping out chicken oysters.

The curve of the blade is dictated by the rocking motion that's key to the Western style of chopping – the point of the blade rarely leaves the board – but it's noticeable that, as Japanese and Chinese knives have gained acceptance, Western chefs have begun to favour wider blades that enable a more 'up-and-down' chopping style.

BONING KNIFE

BLADE LENGTH: **130MM**
OVERALL LENGTH: **240MM**
WEIGHT: **99G**
MANUFACTURED BY: **THIERS-ISSARD SABATIER**
MATERIALS: **HAND-FORGED CARBON STEEL, BEECHWOOD
PRESSURE-TREATED WITH EPOXY**
COUNTRY OF ORIGIN: **FRANCE**
USES: **BONING MEAT OR POULTRY**

ALTHOUGH JOINTS CAN BE BONED with a regular chef's knife, it can be tough on the blade. Boning requires a certain amount of sawing, 'keyhole' working and occasional use of leverage on the blade. Boning knives, therefore, are usually shorter and ground to be much narrower across the blade – usually the bolster sticks out further than the edge.

Chefs rarely work from whole carcasses – meat arrives from the butcher already broken down, so the boning knives in their rolls are rarely beyond 7 inches in length. It's all you need for preparation of joints and birds for cooking. Butchers' boning knives, covered elsewhere (see page 143), are of more terrifying size and infinite variety.

The chef's boning knife will be expected to work down the thighbone of a lamb leg without much collateral damage to the meat, and have enough stiffness in the blade to enable tough tendons to be cut with the extreme tip. Yet the blade that can 'tunnel-bone' a lamb leg will also serve to remove the oysters from a chicken carcass or shape up a standing rib roast.

This is a carbon-steel Sabatier version with a rosewood handle. The handle here has been impregnated with resin, so it will have a much longer life than older-style plain wood.*

---

* Old wooden handles can be revitalised by standing them in a jar of kitchen oil overnight.

FILLETING KNIFE

....

BLADE LENGTH: **150MM**
OVERALL LENGTH: **250MM**
WEIGHT: **110G**
MANUFACTURED BY: **THIERS-ISSARD SABATIER**
MATERIALS: **HIGH-CARBON STAINLESS STEEL, BEECHWOOD
PRESSURE-TREATED WITH EPOXY** ·
COUNTRY OF ORIGIN: **FRANCE**
USES: **FILLETING OR SKINNING MEAT, FISH OR POULTRY**

....

RESTAURANTS USUALLY TAKE DELIVERY of pre-cut fillets of large fish so a chef will only regularly fillet smaller ones. For these the flexible filleting knife is perfect for the job. Flexibility means that the flat of the blade runs along the ribs with no waste of flesh and little chance of nicking the soft bones. The same technique, flexing the flat of the blade against the waste material, means that the flexible filleter is also a brilliant skinning knife and can work flat against the surface of meat, removing silverskin or tough connective material. It's also terrific for poultry, which requires a more delicate approach.

The filleting knives used by fish professionals are in a different league. There are now machines that can fillet fish well but for centuries it has been a manual skill, each fish individually cut in almost inconceivable quantities by skilled men and women. A fishing fleet returning from weeks at sea could arrive with hundreds of tons of catch that would need to be filleted for salting within hours if it wasn't to spoil. A trawlerman or a herring girl would have no time for the careful surgery of the chef and different, tougher tools evolved.

For maximum flexibility, the kitchen fillet knife will almost certainly be made from a different steel to the knives in the rest of the roll.

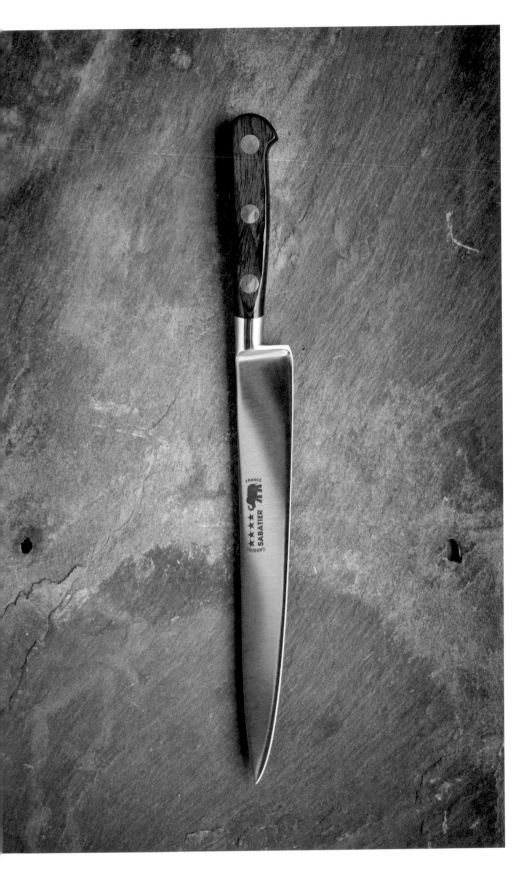

ON CUSTOM KNIVES

PEOPLE OFTEN ASSUME that a chef will commission a special knife in order to achieve a better 'balance' or 'weight'. Actually, the style of knife usually dictates whether the bulk of the weight is in the blade or the handle and, as it is 'locked' to the hand in use, it's almost impossible for any special 'tailoring' to improve or speed up your knife work. The centre of gravity is effectively immaterial. The shape of the blade matters but, as we've established that the blade changes to fit the user and the user changes to fit the blade, this kind of 'technical' bespokery is largely hokum. But the lure of the personalised, 'custom' knife is powerful.

Here in the UK, our culture of knifemaking is in its very early beginnings. Yes, there have always been a few people out there making broadswords for fantasists or hobbit halberds, but it's only recently that a very few have begun custom-making knives for cooks. Many of the knifemakers are cooks themselves and the blades they fashion are made to be used.

In other parts of the world though, places with a culture of hunting, fishing and of the private ownership of weapons, knifemaking is more developed. The knife in the picture is a custom-made filleting knife for a fisherman, made by Guillaume Cote in Ontario, Canada. The handle is made with pine cones set in resin and then highly polished to resemble fish scales, the pommel end is shaped into a symbolic fish skull.

Though the knife would do sterling work on a boat or at the side of a river, gutting a freshly caught salmon, it's too beautiful, and way too costly, for such use. One could spend pages debating the exact point at which a piece of craftsmanship becomes a piece of art but it's fair, I think, to suggest that this knife was made at the very least to be looked at and appreciated as much as used. Though some knifemakers will take commissions for blades made to a customer's exact designs, many now prefer to execute in their own unique style, a further push into the area of the art object.

In the US, knife collecting is a popular pursuit. The work of established star knifemakers like Bob Kramer or Murray Carter and rising stars like Doghouse Forge, NHB KnifeWorks, Chelsea Miller or Bloodroot Blades is so desirable that they have waiting lists months or years long, some even auctioning their work, with prices beginning at hundreds or thousands of dollars 'per blade inch'.

This is complicated territory. I'm not sure I like it when a knife drifts away from form following rigorously on function and yet... though my computer and phone keep perfect atomic time, I still wear a wristwatch that loses a few seconds a month; though I could buy an efficient modern SUV, I drive an ancient 'classic' car. These things are more beautiful than they are efficient, so I can appreciate that for some people the best knives are so lovely that ownership alone is pleasure enough. Occasionally, even I encounter knives so exceptional, so beautiful that it's almost enough just to stare at them, though often they are most affecting when they are old and worn down by a productive life.

Ultimately, though, the pleasure for me is in a relationship which can only really develop by using the knife as often as possible, caring for it and maintaining it. It might be nice to have a locked case, or even a room, where I could sit quietly and appreciate the work of great makers, but, every now and then, I'd have to take down even the most priceless blade in my collection, carry it to the kitchen and chop some onions.

BOB KRAMER

Bob Kramer is widely accepted as the most important culinary knifemaker in America. He originally trained as a chef but became obsessed with knives and set about learning to make them. Kramer was accepted into the American Bladesmiths Society,* a body of around 120 top craftsmen who, until his arrival, had largely specialised in decorative fighting or hunting knives, and soon became something of a cult figure to famous chefs and wealthy foodies. For a while Kramer merely had a three-year waiting list for a knife – as do many of the better makers – but he now makes fewer, even more beautiful pieces at his studio in Washington State and sells them only by online auction.

Some of the best chefs in the US own Kramer knives and if that's the league you want to play in, you'll need to sign up at his website, undergo a brief credit check and then wait to be informed of an opportunity to bid. At the time of writing, Kramer was auctioning a staggeringly beautiful 10-inch *gyuto* with a handle made of spalted box elder and a Damascus blade forged with iron from a meteorite recovered from Campo Del Cielo in Argentina. The blade was differentially hardened by heating while parts of it were coated in clay.

It was a hotly contested sale and I have to confess that, weakling that I am, I bottled out when the price went north of $43,000.

---

* According to Kramer's biography, 'The test required building a 10-inch Bowie knife made of 300+ layers of steel. This one knife had to cut through a 1-inch free hanging rope in one swing, chop through a two-by-four twice, shave a swatch of arm hair (after the two-by-four) and, finally, bend the blade at a 90 degree angle without the blade breaking. If you succeed, then you submit five flawless knives (including a 15th-century Quillion dagger, a very difficult knife to make) to a panel of judges.' After all that, something for chopping carrots must have been a breeze.

OFFICE/PARING KNIFE

BLADE LENGTH: **100MM**
OVERALL LENGTH: **200MM**
WEIGHT: **59G**
MANUFACTURED BY: **DÉGLON SABATIER**
MATERIALS: **STAINLESS STEEL, THERMOPLASTIC**
COUNTRY OF ORIGIN: **FRANCE**
USES: **VEG PARING, PEELING, DELICATE SLICING**

THE PARING KNIFE or *couteau d'office* usually has a blade length of 10 centimetres or less and is shaped like a slender chef's knife. It has three main actions. Like the chef's knife it can be used to chop, but just really tiny things. This makes it the go-to blade for shaving garlic into transparent slices '...so thin they liquefy in the pan. It's a very good system.'* The tip of the blade is great for cutting and teasing out small blemishes in fruit, the hard bits in a fresh peeled pineapple or the hulls of strawberries; or the whole cutting edge can be used in the same way as the turning knife – always pushing the vegetable on to the blade – to peel vegetables.

Possibly because they are a little tricky to keep sharp, but more likely because they are constantly getting stolen in busy kitchens, fewer and fewer chefs seem to keep an expensive office knife these days. It has been the first professional knife type to be replaced by mass-produced knives – with razor-sharp but short-lived blades and brightly coloured, plastic handles, priced so cheaply that they are regarded as disposable.

Personally, I'm of the opinion that a classic 'office knife' is worth the effort of looking after, particularly where workmates are trustworthy. Cheap, disposable knives are brilliant, but be aware that every time you use one, a tiny part of your soul will die.

---

* I know Paulie Cicero used a razor blade in *Goodfellas*. But he was a good enough cook that he would have used an office knife if the screws had let him have one.

TURNING KNIFE

BLADE LENGTH: 70MM
OVERALL LENGTH: 180MM
WEIGHT: 61G
MANUFACTURED BY: J. A. HENCKELS
MATERIALS: ICE-HARDENED STAINLESS STEEL, THERMOPLASTIC
COUNTRY OF ORIGIN: GERMANY
USES: VEG PEELING, TURNING AND CARVING

TURNING OR 'TOURNÉ' is rapidly becoming one of the lost kitchen arts. Few diners are truly happy to see their vegetables carved into controlled little shapes – it militates against modern ideas of freshness and authenticity – and yet, as the perfect boiling time for a vegetable is a function of its density and thickness, the practice of carving each one to such a shape and size that they all cook perfectly together is not quite as silly as it first sounds.

The turning knife is designed, uniquely, to cut towards the hand. It is held curled in the fingers with the thumb used to push the vegetable on to the blade. It's vital to get this right because, by reversing the action and pulling the blade back towards your thumb, you'll almost certainly end up having to explain to an overworked doctor precisely why you're bleeding all over her nice, clean Emergency Room. By turning a length of carrot in one hand and taking identical crescent-shaped strokes across it with the curved blade, the poor sous chef whittles a sort of long, regular oval shape which looks spectacular on the plate.

To modern cooks this must seem like an immensely wasteful practice, but bear in mind that any kitchen that has enough sous chefs to turn vegetables – and customers rich enough to pay for them – is almost certainly making stock in industrial quantities, so no peelings or trimmings would be wasted.

The tip of the turning knife can also be used to cut even grooves in the cap of a mushroom to create *champignons tournés*, or fluted mushrooms. When Shirley Conran said that life was too short to stuff a mushroom, she had only touched the very tip of the possibilities of true time-wasting.

STEAK KNIVES

BLADE LENGTH: **133MM**
OVERALL LENGTH: **254MM**
WEIGHT: **88G**
MANUFACTURED BY: **UNKNOWN**
MATERIALS: **X50CROMOV15 STEEL,
DUPONT 'DELRIN'**
COUNTRY OF ORIGIN: **GERMANY**
USES: **TABLE SETTING FOR MEAT OR GAME**

FOR CENTURIES we carried knives as personal accessories, everyday tools and sidearms. There was no point in having knives at table when everyone – men, women and children – carried perfectly serviceable blades at their belts. It was at aristocratic tables, then, that the first purpose-made 'eating' knives appeared; decorative, usually expensive to better display the host's wealth, often with rounded ends and blunt edges. Fine for dividing soft cooked food and pushing it on to a fork but, perhaps most importantly, useless as an offensive weapon.

It's only in more recent years that the steak has become a high-status food, as symbolic of wealth as finely carved and sauced meat. Big, juicy, seared and properly near-raw at the centre, and needing to be dealt with at table. It's actually impossible to cut a steak with the kind of knife you'd use to cut and push refined, prepared foods. We need the 'steak knife'.

This pair is sold by Donald Russell, an extremely high-class butcher in Scotland, famous for spectacularly good steaks. The knives are made to the same standards as kitchen knives and are deliberately designed to have many of the same visual cues.

Steak knives don't need to match your forks, they need to look like they can honour a serious piece of meat and so need to appear both reassuringly expensive and brutally efficient.

THE NAT GILPIN
COLLECTION

NATHANIEL GILPIN was the head chef at The Silver Cross in Whitehall from 1920 to 1950. Today it's an imposing traditional boozer, popular with tourists, but when Gilpin was in charge it served substantial, high-quality food to members of parliament and civil servants. It would be hard to imagine a more stereotypically British dining environment; solidly Victorian, at the very heart of 'The Establishment' and yet, somehow democratic. Unlike the surrounding private members' clubs, pubs and chop houses, The Silver Cross served all social classes. In a photograph taken in 1932 for *Country Life* magazine (see page 72), Gilpin stands behind the Luncheon Buffet Bar flanked by his assistant Fred Sadler (right), proudly displaying a spread of hams, turkeys and cooked crabs and lobsters.

Beginning as a Royal Navy Officer Steward 3rd Class during the First World War, Gilpin worked his way up through the catering trade. He favoured Sheffield blades and, though often partially obscured by sharpening, you can still detect the ghost trademarks of once great British cutlery brands on his knives: Mexea and Co., Beehive, Wm. Gregory 'All Right', Butler. Some of these marks are from companies already defunct when Gilpin began cooking, so we can imagine that he may have inherited them from older cooks.

The long, straight knives probably began as ordinary slicers, with parallel-sided blades a centimetre or two across. Having a knife sharpened to just a few millimetres in width, though, looked good in front of the customers. Even today, if you order a salt beef sandwich, or good smoked salmon carved to order, the counterman will use a knife that's sharpened almost to the point of non-existence. It reassures the customer to see a tool of the trade so obviously well used and cared for: 'Look how thin and sharp that old knife is, he must really know what he's doing.'

Some of the knives with chunkier, more substantial handles would have been more like thick butcher knives in their original form but, with admirable thrift, Gilpin has kept them going through other useful incarnations in the kitchen. One or two have curved backs, indicating that they may have functioned as boning knives.

Unpacking the knives and arranging them for photography is a powerfully affecting experience. There is always something moving in handling someone's tools – the feeling that they have sat in someone's hand every moment of their long working lives imbues them with emotional weight. But there is more in these knives,

one begins to imagine more. Do the thin carvers reveal a pride in a skill that Gilpin enjoyed displaying? There is a flash of the swashbuckler in their absurdly rapier-like shape. Some knives have stayed in use beyond the point when their original shape was gone. Does that imply a kind of stern thrift?

Nat Gilpin passed his knives to his grandson, Scott Grant Crichton, who also went on to a distinguished career in catering, beginning as a commis chef at the Baron of Beef in Gutter Lane in the City of London in 1968 and working later in hotels and on private yachts. Individually the knives are beautiful; as a collection they form a comprehensive memorial to a working chef.

廠

請認商標 英漆刀廠

獻貢新最

精求益精

刀鋼蓮特　EXTRA

牌球地虎雙

利鋒別特・用耐別特

（口街

七三四

（C8～C

如蒙惠顧

請留意焉

ON CHINESE KNIVES

··

CHINESE AND FRENCH are the two great cuisines of the world, perhaps so exciting because they are so very different at such a fundamental level. Each focuses on different ingredients, different physical sensations in eating and different philosophical beliefs about benefits of various foods, but they differ most noticeably in the utensils used at table. Fine French cuisine is all about knives and forks while the Chinese have been eating with chopsticks since 1000 years before Christ. It's thought that the sticks originated as an improvised method for moving hot food in pots while cooking but soon became the polite way to eat.

There is a theory that the chopstick's popularity was supported by elements of Confucianism, in particular the belief that sharp, warlike instruments such as knives had no place at the civilised dining table. With no one in the dining room equipped to cut their food into bite-sized pieces, it becomes imperative that the food be properly cut up before serving (it is a bonus that food cut like this cooks more quickly over less fuel).

Chinese cuisine, therefore, relies entirely on the use of the knife in the kitchen... and a unique knife it is. The *cai dao* is sometimes referred to as a 'cleaver' because that's the closest thing to it in our knife rolls, but in fact it is a similar tool to the French chef's knife – just a lot wider and without a point.

A *cai dao* is bewilderingly light in the hand as the blade, though unexpectedly large and often with a coarse-looking rough surface finish, is actually very slender. It can be used for up-and-down vertical chopping but also rocked or pushed/pulled like any other kitchen knife. A Chinese cook will always use a cutting block, usually made of wood and standing taller than a Western chopping board – at least 9 centimetres high. Historically this would have been a tree trunk or slice of log and crucially, it allows a different kind of cut. Using a raised block means that the cook's hand is clear, his knuckles can't hit the benchtop and he is able to flip the *cai dao* on its side and slice horizontally.* The raised cutting surface is so important to the use of the *cai dao* that it should almost be considered a part of the knife.

---

* A Western chef can make this horizontal cut but to do so he has to drag his board to the edge of the bench and lean awkwardly. The alternative is to use a blade that will flex to horizontal while still keeping one's knuckles clear of the board. This is probably why such knives have only appeared in Western kitchens in recent years as flexible steel has become available.

If you ever get a chance to watch a good Chinese cook, butcher or fishmonger work, it's a remarkable choreography of entirely unique knife strokes which look immensely rapid and brutal but are in fact subtle and calculated. The same blade that will take the bony and cartilaginous head off a fish will then be used to scale it, gut it, fillet, slice it into transparent slices and fan them on a plate. It's said that in more rural environments the *cai dao* is even used to split the firewood used to cook on. If you're ever lucky enough to experience Peking duck presented with all the tableside ceremony, a chef will carve the cooked duck off the bone with deft strokes of the tip of a *cai dao*; and, though the flat of the blade can be used to smash garlic or ginger to a pulp, the sharp heel is just as often used to peel them. Perhaps the best indication of the delicacy of the *cai dao* is the term for their finest 'chiffonade' cut: 'silver pine needle'.

The second knife of the Chinese chef is a cleaver. A proper, heavy one with a thick spine and a broad wedge-shaped grind. It's kept sharp enough to be capable of cutting through bone – many Chinese preparations involve cutting meat into small pieces but retaining part of the bone for texture and flavour. And because the cook is so adept with the *cai dao*, some of its duties cross over.

For some reason the *cai dao*, for all its history, versatility and just total coolness, has not caught the imagination of Western chefs as much as the specialised knives of Japan. This is a pity because good examples are available through Chinese stores for very little money and are an absolute treat to work with.*

---

* Maintain a Chinese blade like any other by cleaning it with a damp cloth and oiling it lightly but be very careful never to immerse it completely while washing. Water can work itself into the ferrule and up into the handle where it rots the wood and rusts the tang. You really don't want the blade of your chopper snapping off the handle mid-swing.

CAI DAO

BLADE LENGTH: **206MM**
OVERALL LENGTH: **310MM**
WEIGHT: **281G**
MANUFACTURED BY: **LEUNG TIM CHOPPERS CO.**
MATERIALS: **LAMINATED STEEL, HARDWOOD**
USES: **GENERAL PURPOSE**

LEUNG TIM CHOPPERS are regarded as some of the best in the world. Compared with Japanese- and German-made blades they appear functional to the point of rustic, with irregular forging marks on the flat sides of the blades, rough-cut backs and edges, and tangs thrust right through the handles and roughly hammered flat at the back. They are not something that could, on the face of it, be considered elegant and yet there's something incredibly appealing about their complete fitness for purpose. I have enormous sympathy for a maker who's obviously thought, 'what the hell is the point of polishing this thing up and giving it a finish like a piece of jewellery when it's going to be used hard, by an artisan cook, every day?' It couldn't be further from the aesthetic of the Japanese knife and yet a Leung Tim *cai dao* is beautiful in the same way that an old blacksmith's hammer is – it arrives with a lifetime of patina and dripping with butch chic.

The blade length is pretty much the same as the standard Western chef's knife and weighs only a couple of grams more. There's a slight curve on the blade which allows for a rocking–chopping action, and because it takes a beautifully sharp edge easily, you very quickly find yourself using the entire cutting edge, from heel to tip, for all kinds of surprisingly delicate tasks.

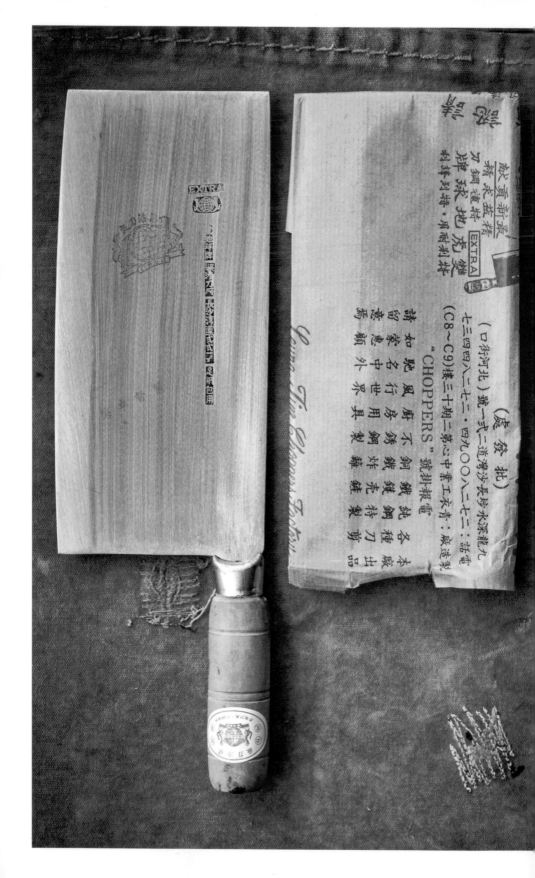

TRADITIONAL CHINESE CLEAVER

BLADE LENGTH: **218MM**
OVERALL LENGTH: **330MM**
WEIGHT: **538G**
MANUFACTURED BY: **LEUNG TIM CHOPPERS CO.**
MATERIALS: **STAINLESS STEEL, HARDWOOD**
USES: **HEAVY BUTCHERY AND FISH WORK WHERE
BONES NEED TO BE CUT**

THE TRADITIONAL CHINESE CLEAVER is a heavy beast. Because the blade is used with more force it needs weight, which would soon damage a delicate edge, so it's ground into a wider wedge. This means there's no point in all the careful laminating that makes for a sharpenable core, so the cleaver is forged out of a single slug of metal.

This traditional cleaver has little refinement and, though a regular user would get used to it, the cutting force is applied towards the back of the blade where most of the weight seems to sit. And it's some serious weight. The cleaver is a monster to heft, the spine a beefy 6 millimetres thick and, if well maintained, quite capable of chewing through the heftiest of beef bones in a few swift strokes.

CHINESE CLEAVER
(LIGHT, FRONT-WEIGHTED)

BLADE LENGTH: **182MM**
OVERALL LENGTH: **285MM**
WEIGHT: **454G**
MANUFACTURED BY: **LEUNG TIM CHOPPERS CO.**
MATERIALS: **HIGH-CARBON STEEL, HARDWOOD**
USES: **FUNCTIONS AS A DOMESTIC CHOPPER FOR LIGHT BONES, CAN PERFORM SOME OF THE FUNCTIONS OF A CAI DAO**

THIS MORE EVOLVED VERSION of the cleaver is a smart hybrid. The blade is laminated, the edge sharp and though the spine is thick for strength, a concave profile to the face means that the blade remains light. Cleverly, though, the blade shape widens to the front so the centre of gravity is moved towards the tip. It's a brilliant adaptation. The extra weight upfront increases the leverage when the chopper is swung and alters the balance so the whole thing feels more like a *cai dao* in terms of maneuverability. It doesn't feel quite right for fine work but, given the brief – a tough, all-round tool for working cooks – the front-weighted cleaver certainly does the job.

HENRY HARRIS

HENRY HARRIS IS ONE of London's best-loved and respected chefs. His training was classical and his CV lists some of the most influential kitchens in the country. His knowledge of cooking technique, ingredients and food history is second to none but his attitude to his knives borders, by his own admission, on the obsessive. Henry has carefully preserved every knife he has ever owned and worked with professionally, and can tell the story of each.

These days Henry can afford the knives he wants and has some expensive and exclusive beauties in his knife roll but, possibly uniquely among collectors, he uses every knife he buys for both work and pleasure and has the talent to test them to their limits.

Henry understands knives as deeply as he loves them and seems comfortable talking about the relationship...

HH: When I left Leith's School of Food & Wine in '83, the chef's roll contained the proper original Sabatier carbon-steel knives. I'd always looked at blunt knives at home and at my father flicking the sharpening steel up and down and not really making them any sharper, so when I first got them I remember thinking, 'God, it's remarkable. Sure, I might not be able to cut an onion because the blade goes black – but when I use this very coarse sharpening steel you can almost see it reaming off either side of the edge and it gets sharp again.' I guess that was the start.

Once I started working in a restaurant I bought a couple of stainless-steel knives which always appear to be a lot more practical. I was immediately frustrated because once that edge has gone the first time you really struggle. They're great workhorse tools, and they served me very well, but I was always thinking there's something not quite right about them.

I spent years sort of satisfied with the knives I'd got and then my wife bought me a *nakiri* from Jay Patel. It came with a little leaflet explaining that it was 'Aogami #2 Blue Paper steel', and I thought, here's something I can waste days over, trawling the internet and looking at stuff. Then as I started working with the knives the world opened up – it was so much more pleasurable.

I'd been worried about knives being too light, but in fact the right knife doesn't have to weigh a lot. It's about strength and how hard you can make that cutting edge without making it brittle. And then you begin to learn how much better a truly sharp blade works with the ingredients. You slice an onion and you don't cry; you cut a piece of fish or meat and that cut surface looks quite different. Smooth, pristine and beautiful.

I don't play the violin or the cello, but when I'm trying to show someone how to use a knife I ask them to think of someone playing the violin and them drawing the bow across the strings to make one note. Draw it through. The knife will do it. If your knife is sharp it will do the whole thing. I tasted something in the kitchen the other day where you could tell from eating the chopped onions that they'd used a blunt knife. There was a toughness to them because they'd been torn rather than chopped.

It started almost ten years ago and I just started collecting at probably a faster rate than I should have done.

And I guess I'm a hoarder. The old blades? Well, they're useless... and they're not. I sharpen up some of the original Sabatiers and they're not a bad knife. What I'm annoyed about is that I haven't got rid of the various cheap knives. I suppose it's a bit like the way I struggle to get rid of cookery books. I've got some really bad cookery books, but if someone's gone to the trouble to write about food – even if I disagree with their point of view – I think it requires investigation and that aids your progression and maturity as a cook. It's the same way with knives. The experience with them, good or bad, all helps to develop your character and skills.

There is only one knife that I really dislike as a knife, and, I suspect, for the keen non-professional home cook, its the most popular knife: the *santoku*. I hate it as a knife. I suppose if you were going camping it would be a useful knife to have, because it's multipurpose. I go for the right knife for the job. When I'm cooking I make sure that they're there, in the same way that a carpenter has his rack on the wall or his box with his tools laid out. I wipe the knife, put it down and pick up the next appropriate one. The *santoku* is good at doing many things but to me it's a compromise. It will do the job but it won't be as good a job as if I had the right knife there, which I probably would anyway. If that makes sense.

These days I'd rather have a *nakiri*, a *gyuto*, some kind of carving knife, either Japanese or Western and something small. That is probably all I need.

I've met knife collectors who spend thousands of pounds on beautiful knives that were designed to skin animals, to gut animals, to cut them, slice them, portion them, to turn vegetables into suitable shapes to cook beautifully... and they put them in a cabinet. They probably wouldn't sharpen their knives and they're worried about getting marks on the blades.

I think a knife comes with the spirit of the person who's made it and he opens it up for the user. The knife has a spirit imbued into it by the bladesmith that enables the user to give it character, so I almost look forward to the moment I get a first scratch on the blade. My Murray Carter *gyuto* has got some scratches on it but I know exactly where they are and how they came about. It was because I was distracted, it was on a bone, it was on another piece of metal. But they are there, they are part of my knife. And as I use it and sharpen it, over the years, that blade will change shape slightly – but I bought it to use it and so the real pleasure in owning it is in cutting, slicing and carving.

JAPANESE KNIVES

ON JAPANESE KNIVES

···

JAPANESE SUPREMACY in the manufacture of kitchen knives came about almost certainly by the unintended consequences of a couple of imperial edicts.

In 1868 Japan underwent huge political upheaval in which full power was restored to the Emperor Meiji who, in the period up to the turn of the twentieth century, turned the country from a feudal to a modernised nation.

Four years later it was announced that the Emperor and his family regularly partook of meat. Meat-eating had been largely prohibited in Japan since 675, partly by legal decree and partly as it was taboo in Buddhist belief, though it could be eaten for medical purposes in the belief that it increased physical strength. Aristocrats would occasionally indulge in *yakuro*, ceremonial hunts at which the quarry would be eaten and citizens who could afford to could go to *momonjiya* – specialist animal restaurants.

The Japanese had looked at Western visitors and associated their size and physical strength with the practice of meat-eating so, as part of his attempt to 'civilise' and modernise Japan, the Emperor actively encouraged its consumption. On March 28 1876, the Meiji government issued *Haitōrei*, one of a series of edicts designed to crush the last influence of the feudal Samurai class. *Haitōrei* forbade the carrying of weapons in public and, at a stroke, put swordsmiths with a thousand-year tradition of forging and maintaining exquisite blades, out of work. In a culture that respected the arts of the kitchen almost as much as the arts of war, beautiful culinary knives were an obvious use for the swordsmiths' skills.

The oldest of the Japanese blade shapes is the *deba*, a chopper-style slicer of a similar pedigree to the Chinese *cai dao* but with a point – great for taking the heads off fish and filleting. The second type, the *usuba* is reminiscent of the vernacular and improvised blades of many of the vegetarian cultures of South and East Asia, the simplest possible execution of a straight, sharp cutting edge. There's no need for a point, in fact it's a liability in a busy kitchen, and the best way to use them, entirely different to the Western cooking knife, is without a chopping board, with the vegetable held in the hand.* The third shape is the *yanagiba*, the willow leaf. Where the *deba* chops downwards and the *usuba* turns vegetables in the hand, the long *yanagiba* blade is drawn through boneless meat and fish in a single, long stroke. Though each blade can be used in other ways, each, at its root, is perfectly adapted to one particular cutting style.

---

* This technique is raised to an art form in *katsuramuki*, a rotary cutting technique. Japanese chefs train in knifework by cutting a chunk of daikon (a giant radish) into paper-thin ribbons (see page 98).

Japanese knifemaking centres on the *shokunin* or craftsman tradition – long and formal apprenticeships in which the trainee, even after the completion of the formal relationship with the teacher, continues to work in largely the same style. This patrilineal system of training creates 'schools' of craftsmanship and tends towards regionally characteristic styles. This is a goldmine for the knife geek as you can end up with a half dozen or so confusing descriptors for every blade. It is also part of *shokunin* tradition to do one thing, preferably as simple a thing as possible, with excellence. Where a Western artist or craftsman might want to 'push the boundaries' of his medium or aspire to make great creative leaps forward, the *shokunin* desires nothing more than to spend the rest of his working life doing the same thing, ever closer to the perfection of the way he was taught. It is nothing less than a total inversion – at a deep, culture-wide level – of the notion of what it is to be a creator. The notion of *shokunin* is so specific to Japanese culture that Western writers regard it with a kind of mystic awe, and is why the Japanese state considers some of the knife craftsmen so symbolic of their heritage that they've been named Living National Treasures.

In Sakai, the place near Osaka where the finest knives are still made, *shokunin* work in tiny workshops with complete division of labour – each completing, as perfectly as they can, a single stage in the making of the knife. One man forges, another shapes, another polishes; others create the edge and fit the handle (see pages 117–124).

The *shokunin* also go some way to explaining the huge variety in Japanese knives. Though there are three basic styles, there are numerous variations by region, as each school of craftsmen has evolved along their own lines. There are also variations by trade. The fishmonger and the chef, *shokunin* in their own way, demand infinite variety in the tools of their own trades. There are knives in the styles of different regions but also subtle variations for individual species of fish or particular vegetables.

Perhaps the most important skill the master swordmakers brought to the kitchen knife was that of combining different metals to create strong and sharp blades. A sword blade needed to be hard, in order to hold an edge and cut, but also to be ductile so it could hit another blade and not shatter. The answer was to take a strip of *hagane*, or high-carbon steel, and wrap it in *jigane*, or soft steel. This slug would be heated and beaten to create the basic form of a blade that could combine the ability to carry an edge with resilience. When you're buying a knife today, this will be referred to as *awase*-style, meaning 'joined', or sometimes *kasumi*-style which means 'enfolded'.

Today the outer layers on your knife blade might well be stainless steel – a lot easier to keep shiny in the kitchen than the soft steel of a fourteenth-century sword blade – or it may be sumptuous *suminagashi*, a steel with a pattern created by layering and acid etching that refers to the Japanese art of paper marbling, for which the Western term 'Damascus' is often used.

DEBA

BLADE LENGTH: **105MM**
OVERALL LENGTH: **290MM**
WEIGHT: **239G**
MANUFACTURED BY: **SAKON**
MATERIALS: **MACHINE-FORGED SHIROGAMI STEEL˚, HO
(MAGNOLIA WOOD), BUFFALO HORN**
USES: **FILLETING, SKINNING, BONING AND SLICING
FISH ORIGINALLY, NOW ALSO MEAT**

THE DEBA LOOKS, and initially feels, like a heavy 'chopper'-style blade. It's thick at the spine and doesn't begin to narrow much until the *shinogi* line (see page 130), at least halfway down the blade. There's nothing in the design calculated to minimise weight. Indeed, the heel end of the blade is used as a chopper when removing fish heads. The cook takes a 'hammer' grip on the handle and brings the very back end of the blade down hard on the bone – and usually goes through at a stroke. But that's where things change. Shifting grip so the handle is in line with the forearm and extending the finger along the spine brings the tip end of the blade into play. The *deba* is single-ground – so it's wickedly sharp and zips through skin and scales – and flat-backed, so it glides over rib bones. Suddenly that extra weight isn't a barrier to delicate work; quite the opposite, in fact – it seems to steady the tip.

Some experts sharpen their *deba* in different ways at different places on the blade, with the tip as delicate as a *yanagiba* and the heel with a more robust angle – it's a lovely idea but way beyond most of our day-to-day knife-maintenance skills.

˚ Japanese knife steels are predominantly made by the Hitachi company. The name refers to the paper it comes wrapped in on delivery. These are the types most often used in knifemaking:

Aogami (Blue Paper) series
Aogami #1: High tensile strength, soft enough to be easy to sharpen
Aogami #2: High toughness and edge retention
Aogami Super: Ideal combination of the above

Shirogami (White Paper) series
Shirogami #1: Hardest among the Hitachi steels, higher carbon
Shirogami #2: Tougher than #1 but slightly less hard

Kigami (Yellow Paper) series
A good-quality general tool steel

The *deba* has become a general-purpose kitchen knife in Japanese cuisine and many good everyday examples are forged from a single steel. It is possible, though, to create an asymmetric *awase*-style laminate which brings all the added advantages of a hard-edge/resilient blade to the *deba* shape. This everyday, machine-forged *deba* is very much to my taste, with an uncomplicated simplicity to it – it's probably about right for my skills in cutting and sharpening too – but there are also incredibly beautiful *suminagashi* pattern versions.

There are dozens of types of *deba*, mostly of similar shape and proportions, but in various sizes, some adapted or recommended for particular species of fish. It's possible to argue that the *yanagiba* is structurally identical to the *deba*, except in length and depth, and is just highly adapted for a single-stroke cutting style.

When double-ground, and particularly when fitted with a 'yo'-style handle for the Western market, the *deba* feels and operates very much like a pleasantly hefty classic chef's knife.

DEBA TYPES

AI-DEBA	light *deba*
ATSU-DEBA	heavy-duty *deba*
HON-DEBA	true/original *deba*
KAKO-DEBA	fishmonger's *deba*, thinner blade (also *usudeba*)
KANISAKI-DEBA	*deba* for filleting crustacea and shellfish
KASHIWA-DEBA	flat-blade *deba* for poultry
KATAI-DEBA	*deba* for breaking down fish and meat
KO-DEBA	small *deba* for filleting smaller fish
MIROSHI-DEBA	filleting *deba*
RYO-DEBA	double-ground *deba*
SAKA-DEBA	salmon *deba*
YO-DEBA	*deba* with a Western-style handle and double ground

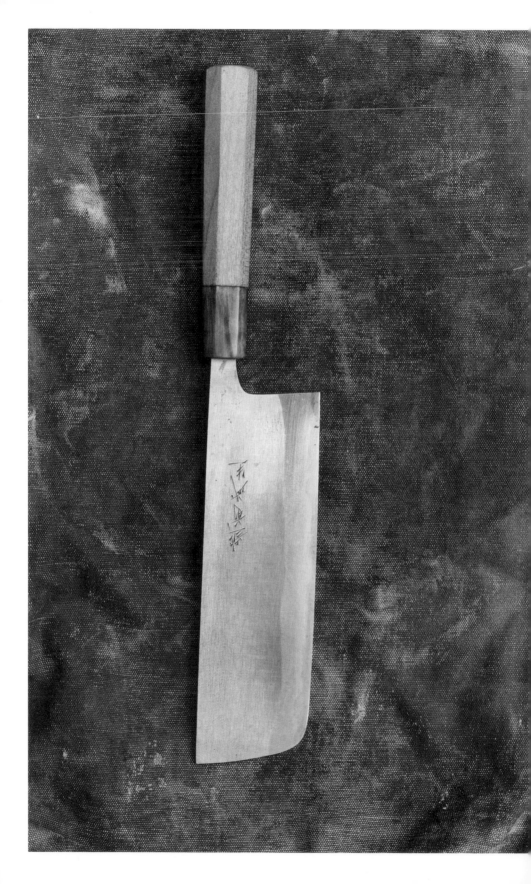

USUBA

BLADE LENGTH: **170MM**
OVERALL LENGTH: **320MM**
WEIGHT: **126G**
MANUFACTURED BY: **SHIRO KAMO**
MATERIALS: **AWASE-FORGED AOGAMI #2 STEEL,
HO (MAGNOLIA WOOD), BUFFALO HORN**
USE: **VEGETABLE CUTTING**

THERE IS SOMETHING UTTERLY DIRECT about the *usuba*. At its simplest it is just the straightest cutting edge – no point, no curve – the most basic expression of a blade, ground only on one side.

Sure there are some refinements. The *kamagata usuba* is a style associated with Osaka, with a quadrant curve between the spine and the tip. The more common *kanto* style is sometimes finished with a one-sided taper towards the square tip – an elegant little refinement that evokes a Japanese-style sword tip but has no culinary function. However, even with these tweaks, the *usuba* is just about applying a dead-straight cutting edge to vegetables.

While meat needs to be placed on a surface and sliced or chopped, a vegetable is often picked up and cut in the hand. The *usuba*, therefore, is light and easy to use in that characteristic 'cut-towards-the-thumb' style, as well as in the same vertical slicing action as the Chinese *cai dao*.

A variety of small *usuba* are available, adapted for slicing particular vegetables or for decorative carving.

ON CUTTING VEGETABLES

....

JAPANESE COOKS have elevated the 'rotary' veg cutting technique to the art of *katsuramuki*. This is where the chef takes a hand-sized length of cylindrical root veg, usually daikon (a large radish) in one hand, lays the flat side of the blade on its surface and, slowly rotating it towards his thumb, reduces the entire thing to one long transparent strip, like unrolling paper. This piece can be folded on itself in layers and then chiffonaded to create the shredded, woolly 'nest' of daikon that often accompanies your sashimi. *Katsuramuki* is one of the techniques apprentice chefs are expected to master, attempting to turn out at least a 2-metre length without mistakes, but for it to work, the blade must be so sharp that no undue pressure is needed – and the cook has to be brave enough to aim that lethal edge right at the most vulnerable part of his own hand.*

Such cutting is usually undertaken with an *usuba*, traditionally the first knife that an apprentice cook will learn to use (as vegetables are cheaper than meat or fish). In rotary cutting the single grind of this blade is an advantage, the flat side gliding the blade parallel to the outer surface of the vegetable, but it also makes it difficult for inexperienced cooks to use for regular slicing. If you're used to a normal, double-ground blade you'll find that the *usuba* wants to drift off to one side and needs constant correcting. The *usuba* is also a little more complicated to keep sharp. The blade shape is so useful, though, that many non-Japanese cooks have either learned to adapt or will buy a *nakiri* – a lighter double-ground *usuba*, designed for the Western cutting style.

---

*   If you're going to try this, and it is worth having a go, I strongly suggest you use a knitted Kevlar cut-resistant glove on the hand that is holding the vegetable. These are easy to find in hardware stores and online and are much cheaper than a cab to A&E.

COMMON CUTS

....

KUSHIGATA GIRI	Wedges (like orange segments) cut from spherical vegetables
WA GIRI	Round slice right across the round or cylindrical vegetable
HANGETSU GIRI	Half of round slice
ICHO GIRI	Quarter of round slice
SEN GIRI	Thin strips (julienne)
HOSO GIRI	Thicker strips (baton)
HYOSHIGI GIRI	Thick baton for root or other hard vegetables
TANZAKU GIRI	Like *hyoshigi* but thinner in one dimension. Rectangles
SOGI GIRI	Paring or shaving cut
MIJIN GIRI	Fine dice
ARAMIJIN GIRI	Coarse dice
RAN GIRI	Irregular shapes created by cutting long thin vegetables diagonally while rolling
ARARE GIRI	Approx. 5mm dice
SAINOME GIRI	Approx. 10mm dice
USU ZUKURI	Single diagonal cut, across grain, turning blade to vertical at the end to create *koba* – defined edge. Paper-thin, transparent slices. Fundamental cut. Used for firm white fish and *fugu* (blowfish)
SOGI ZUKURI	As *usu zukuri* but thicker slices (more than 2.5mm)
HIRA ZUKURI	Thick vertical slices. Common for salmon and tuna from fillet
YAE ZUKURI	Cross-hatched cuts halfway through squid, to tenderise
KAKU ZUKURI	Cubes or dice of soft fish
ITO ZUKURI	Thin, thread-like slices

NAKIRI

BLADE LENGTH: **135MM**
OVERALL LENGTH: **235MM**
WEIGHT: **90G**
MANUFACTURED BY: **BLENHEIM FORGE**
MATERIALS: **AWASE-FORGED HIGH-CARBON STEEL, BOG OAK**
COUNTRY OF ORIGIN: **UK**
USES: **VEGETABLE CUTTING AND PEELING**

THE NAME NAKIRI indicates that the knife is intended for cutting greens. The knife is the same shape as the *usuba* vegetable knife with a flat edge for downwards chopping, but it's not intended for *katsuramuki* rotary cutting of hard root veg so it can take a double grind to the blade.

The *deba* and the *yanagiba* are thick, with a second angle halfway between cutting edge and back – this gives extra strength to the blade. The *nakiri* is thin with smooth, flat faces. Cut a carrot with the wedge-shaped *deba* and it will break away as it slices. Cut with a *nakiri* and you'll have a perfect, smooth edge.

This makes the *nakiri* much easier for Westerners to use than the *usuba*: double-ground blades don't drift off to one side while cutting and are easier to maintain. Perhaps for this reason the *nakiri* has begun to gain ground in Japanese domestic kitchens, much like the *santoku*.

Like the *usuba*, the *nakiri* has regional shape variations – the *kamagata* rounded end is more common in Osaka.

The *nakiri* in the photograph was custom-made for a British cook. The blade is thin, light and very slightly curved, the handle is neither the traditional Japanese *wa* nor the Western *yo* type but a hybrid, thinning towards the heel. It's an incredibly light and delicate knife, small and with a wonderful feeling of flexibility and control.

YANAGIBA

BLADE LENGTH: **260MM**
OVERALL LENGTH: **410MM**
WEIGHT: **194G**
MANUFACTURED BY: **SAKON**
MATERIALS: **HONYAKI (TRUE-FORGED) SHIROGAMI STEEL,
HO (MAGNOLIA WOOD), BUFFALO HORN**
USES: **FILLETING, SKINNING, BONING
AND SLICING FISH**

KENSAKI-STYLE (PICTURED OVERLEAF)
BLADE LENGTH: **260MM**
OVERALL LENGTH: **420MM**
WEIGHT: **205G**
MANUFACTURED BY: **KIKUICHI**
MATERIALS: **AWASE-FORGED GINSANKO STEEL, BUFFALO HORN,
HANDLE UNIDENTIFIED**
USES: **FISH AND MEAT**

THE YANAGIBA or 'willow blade knife' is part of a family of knives used in sushi, sashimi and other fish preparation. By Western standards, the blade is exceptionally long, with professional sashimi cutters using blades over 360mm. The reason for this is that with a longer blade, the cut can be made with a single motion. 'Sawing' or repeated cuts mark the surface of the fish which, in such delicate presentations, should be pristine.

Japanese cooks believe that putting any undue physical stress on the fish during cutting reduces the quality of the finished dish. This requirement for a visually perfect and mechanically efficient cut means that the *yanagiba* is probably the most highly evolved knife type in existence. A *yanagiba* blade can be pushed or pulled through the fish – more weight is applied to a push cut, so it is used when there are scales or small bones to deal with, whereas the delicate final cut on a carefully trimmed fillet is always the more delicate and controllable pull stroke.

Watch a sashimi chef at work and you'll see he begins the stroke by addressing the fish with the heel of the blade and the whole knife pointing upwards at almost 45°. He then pulls the whole length of the blade down and through, an action that can involve moving the whole body.

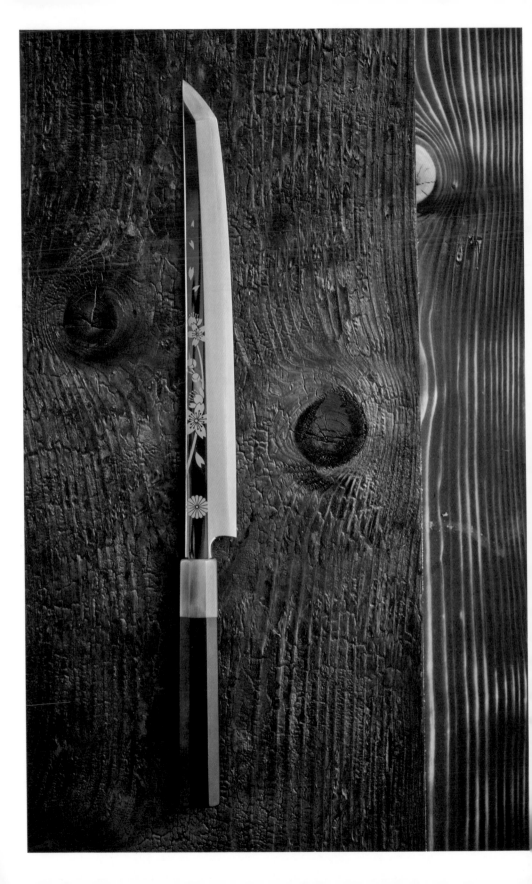

The blade is *honyaki* forged (made from one type of steel) and single ground, which gives better control of the blade angle in skilled hands. The back face of the blade is ground slightly concave, which helps to break suction with the cut face of the fish but also enables the back of the blade to be run over the sharpening stone with only the very edges in contact. The blade is thin and highly polished to reduce friction and therefore the effort required to cut. The single grind means that the cut piece of fish falls away from the main piece more naturally but it also means that left-handed cooks are disadvantaged. Specially made left-handed *yanagibas* do exist, but they are rare and expensive.

Western chefs use a flexible blade to skin fish, bending it so it runs flat against the back of the skin that's pushed flat to the cutting board. The *yanagiba* has no flexibility and will snap easily if used in this way.*

THE KENSAKI-STYLE YANAGIBA is inspired by sword design and sports a rather fetching dropped tip, sometimes called 'tanto'-style after the short sword or dagger of the samurai tradition.

---

* Yes. You have correctly detected a note of bitter and very expensive experience.

TAKOHIKI

BLADE LENGTH: **270MM**
OVERALL LENGTH: **420MM**
WEIGHT: **220G**
MANUFACTURED BY: **SAJI**
MATERIALS: **TRUE-FORGED AOGAMI STEEL
(UNUSUALLY DOUBLE GROUND)**
USES: **NOMINALLY FOR OCTOPUS BUT USED FOR
ALL KINDS OF SASHIMI**

THE TAKOHIKI or 'octopus slicer' is used in exactly the same way as the *yanagiba* but the blade edge is straighter. These are common in the east of Japan and around Tokyo while the *yanagiba* is traditionally found in the west and around Osaka. The fact that two parallel blade styles can evolve for exactly the same purpose does make you wonder what the point of the point is. The slicing action is a long pull and there are few circumstances in which you'd want to use the sharp tip – it would be incredibly hard to control in a foot-long blade. I rather like the idea that this is a quiet reminder of the samurai traditions underlying Japanese knifemaking – that kind of thing appeals to chefs, no matter what culture they come from.

To confuse matters completely there is a type of *takohiki* called a *sakimaru takohiki* which has a straight edge but a gently rounded tip.

HANKOTSU/HONESUKI

BLADE LENGTH: **150MM**
OVERALL LENGTH: **265MM**
WEIGHT: **156G**
MANUFACTURED BY: **KIKUICHI**
MATERIALS: **MACHINE-FORGED 2N CARBON STEEL,
DYED PAKKA WOOD**
USE: **BONING HANGING MEAT**

THE HANKOTSU is the traditional boning knife you'll see in the hands of a Japanese butcher. It is short, thick at the spine and very strong. It can be comfortably held in a 'dagger' grip and used on hanging carcasses where the weight of the meat is used to advantage by the cutter. The sharp tip is excellent at wiggling into complex joints and popping them apart and the first three-quarters of the blade is kept sharp for cutting muscle and removing silverskin. The final quarter of the blade is kept blunt to protect the fingers if they slip past the bolster.

For more general butchery work a Japanese chef will choose a *honesuki* which has a noticeable heel to the blade and some knuckle clearance. A *honesuki maru*, like the one opposite, has a gently curved blade but there are also *honesuki kaku* with a more angular shape. These are ideal for butchering small poultry or rabbits. For larger animal carcasses there is a heavier version of the *honesuki* called a *garesuki*.

Though it's quite specialised in its use, the *hankotsu* has gained favour with Western chefs for its sleek shape and its weight – more substantial than many Japanese blades. It is increasingly common to see them fully sharpened for more general kitchen work.

GYUTO

BLADE LENGTH: **210MM**
OVERALL LENGTH: **350MM**
WEIGHT: **345G**
MANUFACTURED BY: **SAN-ETSU**
MATERIALS: **AWASE-FORGED ZDP-189 STEEL**
USES: **ALL-PURPOSE**

GYUTO TRANSLATES AS 'COW BLADE' and is a comparatively recent arrival in the Japanese chef's roll. Shapes and lengths vary but this is basically the Japanese knifemaker's interpretation of the Western chef's knife. It's double bevelled, deep bellied and narrows to a point but is substantially thinner and lighter than our blade. This example is what the owner describes as 'a very Western *gyuto*' with a *yo*-style rivetted handle and made from ZDP-189 – a specialist high-speed tool steel. The delicate swirling in the Damascus pattern is created by randomly pockmarking the surface with a punch during forging.

This is a truly high-end knife made with Rolls-Royce craftsmanship and Formula One materials. It's also a very good example of how Japanese craftsmanship has adapted to serve wealthy collectors and discerning cooks worldwide. The high-tech steel is amazingly tough, which means that it takes a lot of work to get a good edge on it, but once it's there, it will remain terrifically sharp for a long time. One day, when I'm rich, I'd like one of these. And a vault to keep it in. And a full-time knife-sharpener on my staff...

SANTOKU

BLADE LENGTH: **180MM**
OVERALL LENGTH: **300MM**
WEIGHT: **302G**
MANUFACTURED BY: **SAKURA**
MATERIALS: **AWASE-FORGED R2 101 LAYER DAMASCUS STEEL, EBONY**
USES: **ALL-PURPOSE**

THE SANTOKU is now the knife most commonly used in Japanese home kitchens and has spread all over the world as an ideal general-purpose kitchen knife. In the trainee chef's kit (see page 44) there is often a *santoku* included alongside the chef's knife.

The name is usually translated as 'three virtues' or 'strengths' but nobody can quite agree whether this refers to the ingredients it can be used on – fish/meat/veg – the cutting styles that it can be used for – mince/slice/chop – or the fact that it can serve many of the functions of the three traditional knives, the *yanagiba*, the *deba* and the *usuba*.

As it's a double-ground knife and a Western-influenced shape, the *santoku* is sometimes regarded as a sub-type of the *gyuto* but the story is, I think, more complex. The *santoku* blade shape is a lot less curved along the bottom than a chef's knife, in many ways reflecting the *usuba* and the *cai dao* in use. I believe its rising worldwide popularity has more to do with changing diets and cooking methods. We don't regard French-inspired, meat-heavy cuisine as necessarily the be-all and end-all of cooking any more and are starting to look towards other cultures and to adding more vegetables into our diets. Perhaps it's not surprising then that the time-honoured chef's knife is being supplanted everywhere by a newer, lighter pattern, inspired by more diverse cuisine and biased towards vegetable work.

PETTY KNIVES

....

BLADE LENGTH: **120MM**
OVERALL LENGTH: **228MM**
WEIGHT: **63G**
MANUFACTURED BY: **TADAFUSA**
MATERIALS: **SANMAI HAMMER-FORGED AOGAMI #2 STEEL,
AFRICAN ROSEWOOD**
USES: **GENERAL USE ON VEGETABLES, POULTRY
AND BONELESS MEAT**

BLADE LENGTH: **150MM**
OVERALL LENGTH: **267MM**
WEIGHT: **81G**
MANUFACTURED BY: **TAKAMURA**
MATERIALS: **SG-2 (R2) POWDERED STEEL, PAKKA WOOD**
USES: **AS ABOVE**

....

'PETTY', FROM THE FRENCH 'PETIT', has become a bit of a catch-all term
for a small, double-ground utility knife. Most Japanese manufacturers now make a
petty knife, ranging from 110 millimetres to 150 millimetres in length and shaped like
a slender version of the classic French-pattern chef's knife.

The petty knife is thin, light, has a little flex and is useful for everything from
peeling and paring vegetables to chopping herbs. Though the blade has a pronounced
heel, the whole knife is way too small to wrap your hand around in a 'hammer' grip,
so the blade is usually pinched just ahead of the bolster.

To overcome this lack of knuckle clearance, some manufacturers have come up
with 'offset' petty knives, with a crank in the blade that lifts the handle clearer of the
cutting board. However, they are objects of such abiding ugliness that they have no
place in a well-chosen roll.

Light and manoeuvrable, the smaller petty knives work well for hand-held cutting
away from the chopping board.

Sakai. An industrial town near Osaka-

-Centre of Japanese swordmaking for as long as anyone can remember. Now the home of the world's most desirable kitchen knives.

There is total division of labour. Each part of the knife is made by a different master craftsman, the ultimate specialist...

..Shokunin!

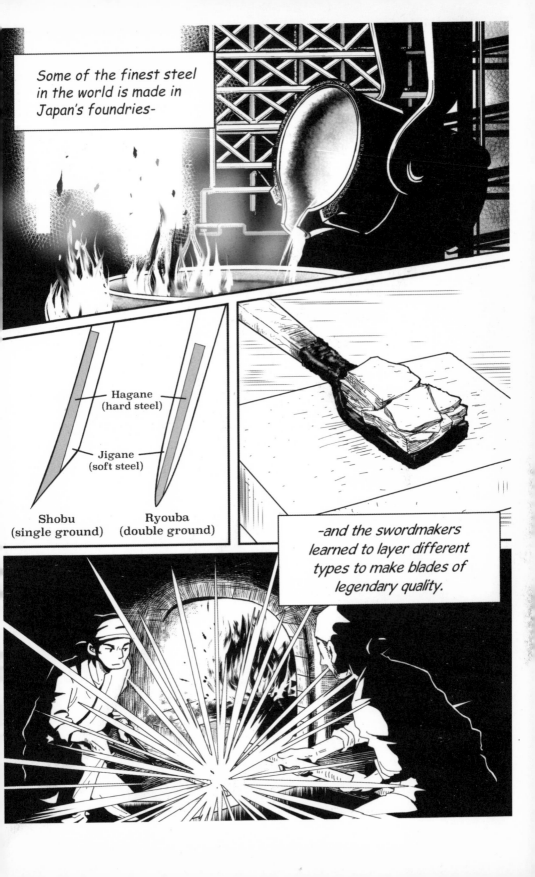

Some of the finest steel in the world is made in Japan's foundries-

Hagane
(hard steel)

Jigane
(soft steel)

Shobu
(single ground)

Ryouba
(double ground)

-and the swordmakers learned to layer different types to make blades of legendary quality.

"Mr Kahasi"
He uses a horizontal wheel then flat stones.

Shtttttng

He knows all the arcane patterns and profiles to make the most effective cutting edge.

裏 Back

峰 (Mine) Spine

表 Front

平 (Hira) Flat

裏スキ (Urasuki) Concave Back

シノギ筋 (Shinogi-suji) Shinogi Line

裏押し (Uraoshi) Burr Removal

切刃 (Kiriha) Blade Path

刃先 (Hasaki) Edge

Flat Ground

Convex

Asymmetrical Semi Convex

Asymmetrical Flat

Compound Bevel

Hollow Ground

Chisel

Chisel with Backbevel

Chisel with Urasuki

Mr あわせ　　Mr きりは　　Mr かはし　　Mr Ho　　Mr E

Mr 角巻　　Mr ひら　　Mr なかご

SUSHIKIRI

BLADE LENGTH: **200MM**
OVERALL LENGTH: **360MM**
WEIGHT: **372G**
MANUFACTURED BY: **SAKAI TAKAYUKI**
MATERIALS: **TRUE-FORGED SHIROGAMI STEEL,
HO (MAGNOLIA WOOD), THERMOPLASTIC**
USES: **ALL-PURPOSE SUSHI SLICER**

SOME TYPES OF SUSHI are made in long bars and cut, just before serving, into single smaller portions. Cutting through the fish ingredients should be done in a single stroke and any nori seaweed should remain dry and brittle, so it's tough to cut with anything but the very sharpest blade. The main rice body has a sticky texture that quickly builds up on the blade, which requires constant wiping with a wet cloth. The job can be done well with a standard *yanagiba* but the *sushikiri* has evolved for the sole purpose of cutting bars or rolls of sushi for the most elegant presentation.

The blade is single ground and light in weight. A complex, multi-layered blade is unnecessary for the singular task and there's no need for the thick spine of the *yanagiba*; the *sushikiri* is thinner, a little like an *usuba*. Most importantly, the blade is long and deep, meaning that the single cut can be made both backwards and downwards.

UNAGISAKI & MEUCHI

BLADE LENGTH: **160MM**
OVERALL LENGTH: **272MM**
WEIGHT: **298G**
MANUFACTURED BY: **SAN-ETSU**
MATERIALS: **AWASE-FORGED SHIROGAMI STEEL,
HO (MAGNOLIA WOOD), BUFFALO HORN**
USES: **SKINNING, BONING, GUTTING AND PORTIONING EEL**

EELS, OR 'UNAGI', have long been popular in Japanese cooking. They are bought alive and must be killed and gutted before cooking.

In many seafood restaurants and fishmongers this is done in front of the customer, as proof of freshness. The eel is dispatched by a swift, shallow cut at the neck, then the head is fixed to the chopping board with the *meuchi*. The fishmonger will then stretch out the body and, using the tip of the blade, split right down the spine of the eel in a single cut, skilfully avoiding damage to the viscera which are then scraped out of the opened and flattened eel with the flat main part of the blade. The spine is removed with a single pass and the eel is ready to cook.

There is almost no set of circumstances in which a Western cook is going to need an *unagisaki* – indeed, it would take years to develop the skills for such a performance even if one needed to – but it's interesting to notice how the simple fish-filleting *deba* has been adapted in this particular case to create such a very specialised tool.

JAPANESE KNIFE DICTIONARY

....

BA/HA	Blade
KIRI	Cutter/cut
HOCHO/BOCHO	Kitchen knife
SHOKUNIN	Craftsman/artisan
SHOBU	Single grind
RYOUBA	Double grind
HONBA TSUKE	Custom sharpening on a new knife
KOBA	Defined edge
KAKU	Square (squared off)
ATSU	Thick or heavy
KO	Small
MIROSHI	Filleting
KATSURAMUKI	Rotary cutting
SAKI	Tearing/breaking
BIKI/HIKI	Pull
KASUMI	Fog, enfold, wrap
AWASE	Joined
YANAGI	Willow
JIGANE	Soft steel
HAGANE	Hard steel
SAN MAI	Steel lamination
SUMINAGASHI	Art of paper marbling
E	Handle
EJIRI	Handle end
KAKUMAKI	Collar/ferrule
AGO	Heel
MUNE or SE	Spine
TSURA or HIRA	Flat
KIREHA	'Blade path' or large bevel
SHINOGI	Line between tsura and kireha
HASAKI	Edge
KISSAKI	Tip end, point
MACHI	Notch where blade meets tang (sometimes visible)

MUNE MACHI	Upper neck notch
HA MACHI	Lower neck notch
HAMON	Line of temper
HADA	Grain pattern
WA	Japan or Japanese-style
YO	Western-style
TARA	Cod
SAKE	Salmon
UNAGI	Eel
TAKO	Octopus
FUGU	Blowfish
BUTA	Pig/pork
SUJI	Tendon
MEN	Noodle

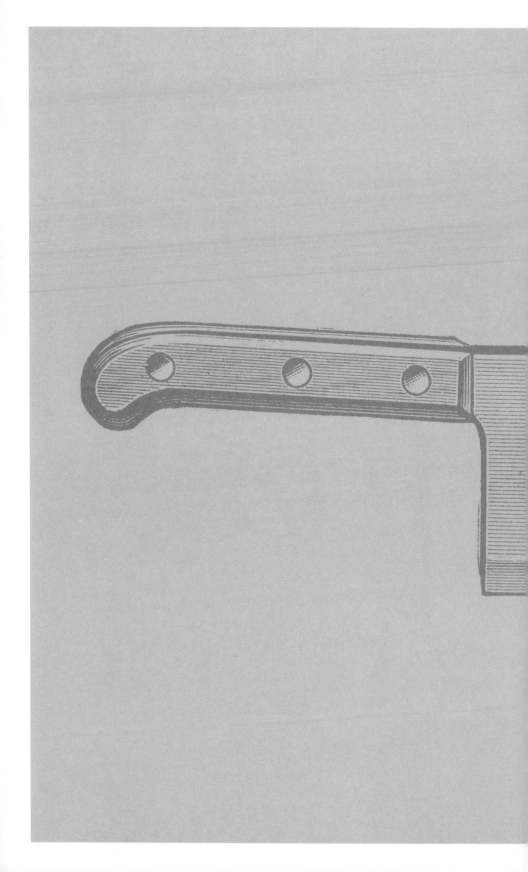

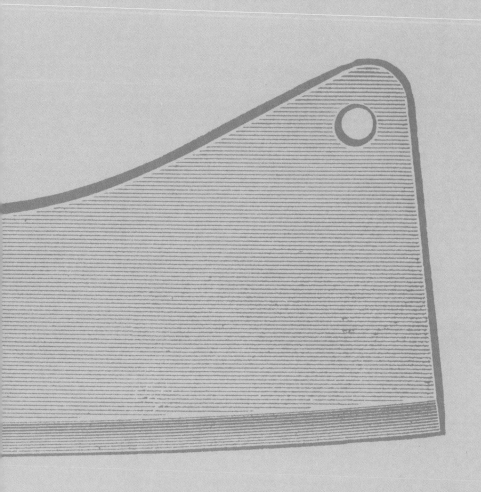

WORKING KNIVES

ON BUTCHER'S KNIVES

···

TECHNIQUES OF BUTCHERY don't just vary internationally. Even across the UK, different cutting plans developed in different regional meat markets. The arcane vocabulary of chumps, chucks, featherblades and fillets historically had subtly different meanings across the country. What has unified British butchery, though, is the joint and the bandsaw. As a nation we favour roasting as the best way of cooking meat and joints; large, almost ceremonial chunks of meat on the bone, have always been the most popular choice over the counter.

The butcher's bandsaw looks and operates just like the woodworker's and enables the butcher to treat a carcass much as a carpenter treats a log. The exterior is neatly dressed and then the meat is sawn into chunks. A classic 'shoulder of lamb' – that fixture of the Sunday dining table – is a neat square package that looks good on the plate but contains at least a dozen muscles, all of different textures, plus bone, gristle and connective tissue, simply chopped into shape. This sounds like a bad thing, but our national cuisine has evolved around the 'joint', and our much envied skill at roasting means that these more heterogenous cuts can be cooked so that the very best of flavour and texture is achieved.

But in other butchery traditions a more sympathetic process has evolved. That of separating the carcass, where possible, into individual muscles or muscle groups by following the 'seams' where the muscles join. Remarkably little kit is required. A short, curved butcher's knife does the initial cutting but the butcher uses the back of it as much as the front, using the blunt edge to scrape where meat adheres to the bone. More unusual is the chainmail glove, not so much, as is often imagined, to protect the opposite hand from the blade but more to provide a sure grip on the meat when pulling muscles free. Seam butchery requires a different set of skills – and often involves relearning for a traditionally trained British butcher – however it can be extremely lucrative. The fore end of a lamb, for example, which might previously have yielded a couple of shoulders, a neck and some mince can be carefully teased out into a dozen or more cuts of varying sizes and textures, simple to cook, economical to buy and delicious to eat. These cuts are often best cooked in the pan rather than the oven and/or stewed in liquids and sauces.

The British butcher's kit, therefore, usually comprises 'steak' and boning knives, with a steel to keep an edge, plus the saw and the cleaver. Other traditions have tools of various patterns that combine the functions of a heavy knife with a light cleaver.

For generations, local butchers were the experts on sharp knives. Many would have a grinding and sharpening wheel on the premises and early books on cookery or household management suggest taking the domestic kitchen knives to the butcher regularly to have them sharpened. Knife practice in the trade though has changed radically with the arrival of the 'diamond steel'.

Where a traditional steel serves only to correct and dress an edge that's been ground on to a knife, the modern 'steel', coated with a fine dusting of abrasive (usually diamond dust) will actually remove metal from the blade.* A diamond steel will quickly put a decent edge on any blade with almost no skill needed, however diamond steeling also eats away the blade at a frightening rate. Though traditional sharpening is still practised by many butchers and taught in apprenticeships, most butchers now use diamond steels and cheaper, mass-produced working knives†, which can be replaced regularly.

---

* See description on page 205.
† The single piece, moulded plastic handle, lacking microscopic cracks or joins where bacteria might lurk, are also greatly preferred by safety regulators.

STEAK KNIFE/SCIMITAR

BLADE LENGTH: 260MM
OVERALL LENGTH: 390MM
MANUFACTURED BY: FORSCHNER/VICTORINOX
MATERIALS: STAINLESS STEEL, ROSEWOOD
COUNTRY OF ORIGIN: USA
USE: CUTTING CLEAN AND REGULAR SLICES
ACROSS BONED MEAT

THE STEAK KNIFE, OR SCIMITAR, is the stereotype of the butcher's knife. It is long in the blade, for cutting across large muscle groups, and, like the *yanagiba*, for creating a fine surface on steaks with fewer pull/push strokes. The blade is massive enough to be wielded as a chopper through small or soft bones and broadens towards the tip, shifting the centre of gravity further from the handle and allowing it to be swung like a hammer. The shape of the tip also fits naturally to a second hand for pushing down evenly through tougher bones or joints.

The name 'scimitar' derives from a curved pattern of sword that pops up throughout Asia and the Middle East and refers to the curve on the cutting edge, which also enables it to be used in a rocking/chopping action to mince.

The steak knife is an interesting example of a knife that has evolved to serve many different purposes. As a single, general tool of the working butcher, particularly in the shop environment, it's ideal – always at hand and turnable to most tasks. Like the chef's knife, the steak knife usually comes in 8-inch and 10-inch blade lengths.

(The example in the photograph began life in a butcher's shop but for the past 30 years has been cutting Chelsea buns at my bakery in Cambridge.)

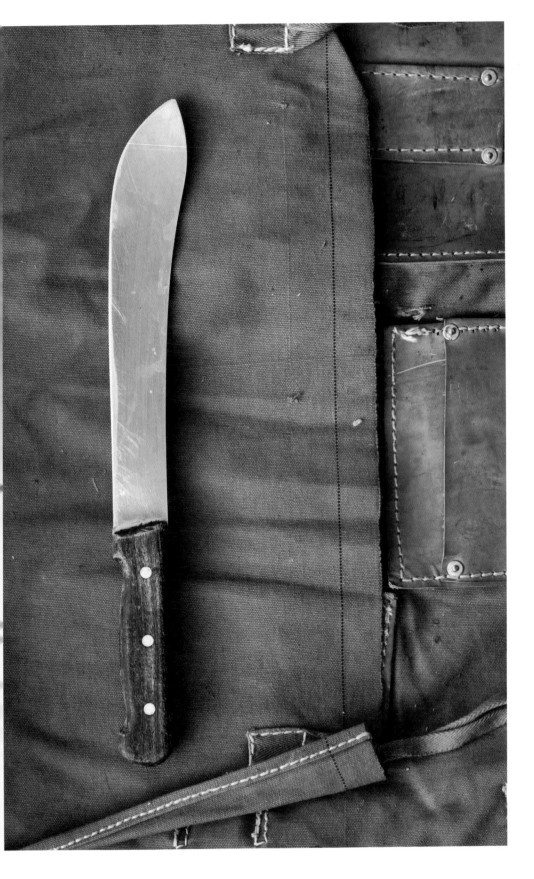

FEUILLE DE BOUCHER

BLADE LENGTH: **270MM**
OVERALL LENGTH: **410MM**
WEIGHT: **902G**
MANUFACTURED BY: **BARGOIN/FISCHER**
MATERIALS: **STAINLESS STEEL, ABS THERMOPLASTIC**
COUNTRY OF ORIGIN: **FRANCE**
USE: **GENERAL-PURPOSE BUTCHERY INCLUDING BREAKING CARCASSES EITHER HANGING OR AT THE BENCH, CUTTING MEAT AND SMALL BONES, DICING MEAT**

THE FEUILLE DE BOUCHER is the French-pattern butcher's knife and cleaver. Though it looks much like our traditional British cleaver in shape, it is actually lighter, sharper and designed to be used in a very different way.

A British or US butcher will use the cleaver on either hanging meat or at the block, cutting with a scimitar to reveal the bone or joint and then swapping to a heavy cleaver with a wide-angle wedge-shaped blade to chop through. The *feuille de boucher* combines the functions of the large knife and the light cleaver; able to go through small joints but also usable to slice steaks or to mince, using the curved tip as a rocking pivot.

The blade of the *feuille de boucher* goes through the handle with a pointed tang, like a Chinese *cai dao*, so to strengthen the joint, for chopping purposes, there are sometimes two extra metal 'cheek pieces' added. With no rivets or exposed joints, the round handle is easier to keep properly clean than the British pattern.

The *feuille de boucher* might be suitable for a sheep carcass but may (and I stress may) not be up to the job of a large cow. For this, a contemporary butcher will use a bandsaw, although traditionally a larger *feuille* would have been used with a longer handle which could be swung, two-handed, like an axe and used to split a hanging carcass down the spine.

FRENCH CLEAVER PATTERNS

FEUILLE DE BOUCHER DE DOS DROIT

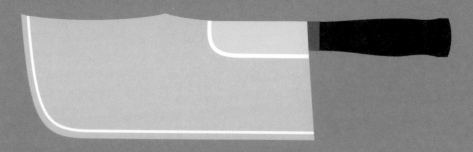

FEUILLE DE BOUCHER DOS CINTRE

FEUILLE DE BOUCHER BELGE

FEUILLE DE BOUCHER SUISSE

COUPERET DE BOUCHER PARISIEN

COUPERET DE CUISINE

BONING KNIFE

BLADE LENGTH: **142MM**
OVERALL LENGTH: **271MM**
WEIGHT: **94G**
MANUFACTURED BY: **FORSCHNER/VICTORINOX**
MATERIALS: **STAINLESS STEEL, ROSEWOOD**
COUNTRY OF ORIGIN: **USA**
USES: **BREAKING DOWN HANGING CARCASSES,
BENCHTOP BONING**

IT'S THE BUTCHER'S BONING KNIFE, in its infinite variations, that's most different from the knife of the same name in the chef's roll.

Because he's cutting constantly, the wholesale market butcher (or the one in the straw hat at your local shop) will sharpen his knives daily and steel them, almost as a nervous tic. Within days of purchase the blades will be changing shape and will probably not have a life expectancy beyond six months.

Where the chef carefully removes small pieces of meat by sliding his knife along the bone, the butcher is removing large, heavy pieces, often from a whole carcass either hanging or on a block. Watch a good butcher at a wholesale meat market and you'll see he constantly changes his grip from the usual position, common to all knife users, to an inverted 'stabbing' hold. Held this way, the thin, stiff blade can get deep in along long bones and nick through ligaments around joints. The joint that has supported over a ton of live beef for the whole of its life is an incredibly tough bit of osteo-engineering; it's not the kind of thing you can separate with the same knife you'd use to take the skin off a lemon sole. The stiff-spined boner has to be rigid enough to force between the massive ball and socket and sharp enough at the tip to nip through the hawser-like tendons that hold them together.

A really skilled butcher 'breaking down' a full carcass uses the boning knife more than any other, locating and exploring the joints with the skill of a surgeon, cutting supporting ligaments here and there and letting the huge weight of the meat work in his favour to separate the pieces.

ON CHANGING SHAPE

···

SHAPE MAY BE ONE OF THE FIRST REASONS you choose a knife. You select the broadly correct shape for the job and then, quite possibly, try several examples, finding the one that feels best in your hand. Initially, it feels 'new' and different, but very quickly, unless you've been unlucky in your choice, your working and cutting style, your grip and your muscle memory adapt. For many, this may be as far as adaptation goes, a one-way process in which you become accustomed to your new knife, but for anyone who works with a knife over a long period, the process has another side – the knife must adapt to fit *you*.

When you buy a knife from a *hamanoya* in Japan, it's common to have it ground to your own cutting style. Some cooks will have a blade single ground from the tip but change to a partial or full double grind as they get closer to the handle. They are aware enough of their cutting style to know that delicate work is done with the tip and belly of the blade, but when hard things have to be cut or joints chopped through, they'll always use the heel. Some Western cooks sharpen a little of the spine, near the tip, for fine boning work (see page 46).

When a knife is used and steeled every day it changes shape constantly and subtly. The commercial butcher, taking down his twentieth beef carcass of the day, is deftly using a blade that is, in places, less than one centimetre thick. When he first started using that blade it was a full-size boning knife, yet it has worn down, adapting to him. He has subtly altered the way he grips and moves it. No one else will feel comfortable holding or working with that knife and the day he has to replace it, he puts himself, for a few days, right back at the bottom of the 'learning curve'.

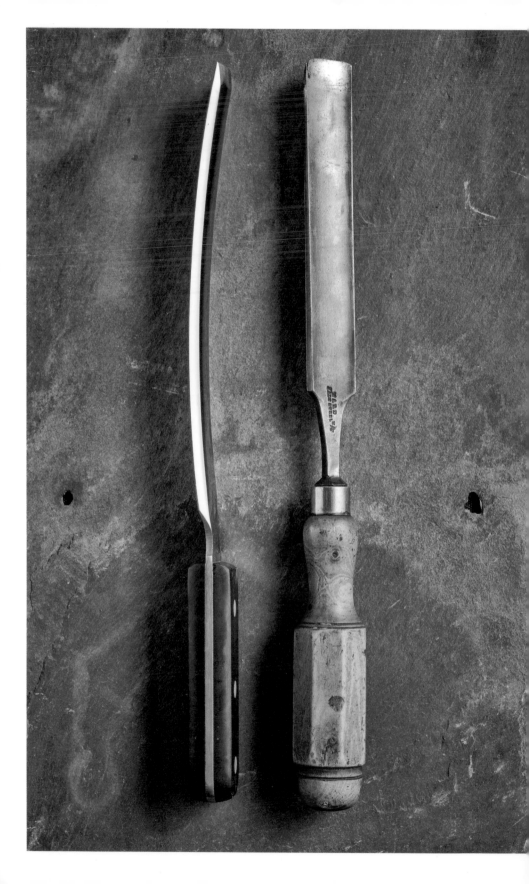

BONING GOUGE

BLADE LENGTH: **235MM**
OVERALL LENGTH: **345MM**
WEIGHT: **346G**
MANUFACTURED BY: **MARTÍNEZ Y GASCÓN**
MATERIALS: **STAINLESS STEEL, THERMOPLASTIC**
COUNTRY OF ORIGIN: **SPAIN**
USE: **DETACHING LARGE BONES WITHOUT PENETRATING
SURROUNDING MEAT**

THE GLORIOUS BONING GOUGE on the left is from Spain, where it would be used in a *jamon* factory or butcher's – slipped along the thigh and shank bones to detach the flesh and remove the bone, readying it for packing in the salt and making ham. It's a beautifully engineered bit of kit, machined in complicated compound curves and sharpened not only along its curved tip but also along both sides.

A boning gouge also makes short work of lamb and venison legs, leaving them easier to carve and providing an interesting little pocket for creative stuffing. Before I found the real thing I had a long and happy relationship with the 1-inch woodturner's gouge on the right, which cost a fiver on eBay.

MORA 9151P FILLETING KNIFE
&
352P GUTTING HOOK

BLADE LENGTH: **151MM** (GUTTING HOOK **66MM**)
OVERALL LENGTH: **290MM** (GUTTING HOOK **252MM**)
WEIGHT: **99G** (GUTTING HOOK **128G**)
MANUFACTURED BY: **MORA**
COUNTRY OF ORIGIN: **SWEDEN**
MATERIALS: **COLD-ROLLED SWEDISH STAINLESS STEEL,**
GLASS-REINFORCED POLYPROPYLENE
USE: **HIGH-VOLUME FISH FILLETING**

THE 9151P is one of a range of knives made by Mora of Sweden for the fishing and fish processing industries. The blade has a little flex and holds a good edge but, most importantly, will stand up to incredibly hard use. The glass-reinforced polypropylene handle is moulded on – so no moisture can get between it and the blade and cause rust – and has a rough finish for better grip in rubber gloves on a heaving deck, covered in freezing salt spray and fish blood. This knife is not designed for delicate kitchen filleting but fast, heavy work on large carcasses.

The gutting hook is a short, sharp blade protected by its own curved spine, which can open the abdomen in a single stroke with no danger of nicking the viscera.

Though both are well finished, there's no element of luxury in materials or design because, for working tools, cost is an important consideration. You may be able to find a supplier who will sell you this kind of knife singly but they're usually packed in boxes of ten. They are perfectly evolved for the job with no effort wasted on pointless gimmickry or unnecessary decoration. As a result, they have a cold, functional beauty all of their own.

GENZO FIELD BUTCHERY KIT

BLADE LENGTH: **130–160MM**
OVERALL LENGTH: **220–300MM**
WEIGHT: **85–120G**
MANUFACTURED BY: **GENZO**
MATERIALS: **440-GRADE STAINLESS STEEL, HIGH VISIBILITY
THERMOPLASTIC WITH 'SANTOPRENE' GRIPS**
COUNTRY OF ORIGIN: **SWEDEN**
USES: **SKINNING, GUTTING AND BREAKING DOWN
CARCASSES IN THE FIELD**

IT IS IN THE NATURE of professional game hunting that the hunter will likely find himself somewhere extremely remote with a large and valuable carcass. If not handled properly very soon after death, most game will deteriorate quickly. The animal must, therefore, be bled, gutted and sometimes skinned 'in the field'. If the hunter has support and transport, the whole carcass can be recovered; if not, prime cuts must be carried out and the remains left for natural scavengers.

The Genzo company in Sweden makes a range of knives for hunters and outdoorsmen. This field butchery kit contains compact versions of a butcher's steak and boning knives, a curved skinner's blade, a gutting or 'gralloching' knife with an inverted blade, along with a steel.

To prevent contamination, the animal should ideally be butchered off the ground, so the kit comes with its own belt and holsters to enable the hunter to work easily on the hanging carcass.

With the possible exception of a length of rope for hanging, this kit contains everything needed to completely butcher a large animal down to manageable cuts, hundreds of miles from the nearest kitchen.

CHAINMAIL GLOVE

BLADE LENGTH: **N/A**
OVERALL LENGTH: **252MM**
WEIGHT: **212G**
MANUFACTURED BY: **JINHUA PREASY MACHINERY CO.**
MATERIALS: **STAINLESS STEEL, NYLON**
COUNTRY OF ORIGIN: **CHINA**
USES: **PROTECTING THE HAND DURING COMMERCIAL CUTTING OPERATIONS AND OYSTER SHUCKING, IMPROVING GRIP IN SEAM BUTCHERY**

OK, I KNOW, it's not strictly a knife but the chainmail glove is becoming a more and more important part of the butcher's kit for an intriguing reason.

Originally, the chainmail glove was used by commercial butchers and fishmongers as protection for the hand not holding the knife – in a long day of dealing with slippery carcasses, it was good to have something on the opposite hand to protect against cuts and this vaguely medieval technology was just right for the job.* (These days there are excellent cut-proof gloves knitted from Kevlar fibres that do this job just as well with less weight.)

The mail glove, though, is gaining popularity as a tool for 'seam' butchery; the style in which individual muscles are separated from the carcass and butchered individually into more homogenous cuts. The technique involves getting a solid grip on the slippery meat and, without the use of the knife, pulling the muscle free. The mail glove is perfect for this. It fits on either hand, affords superb grip, it's well ventilated and, at the end of the day, can be run through the dishwasher.

Both Kevlar and mail gloves are available online for just a few pounds and are definitely worth keeping in your roll, just in case.

---

* The chainmail glove is also an incredibly wise investment if you're planning to open your own oysters. It improves the grip on the shell and will almost certainly save you from disheartening amounts of blood loss.

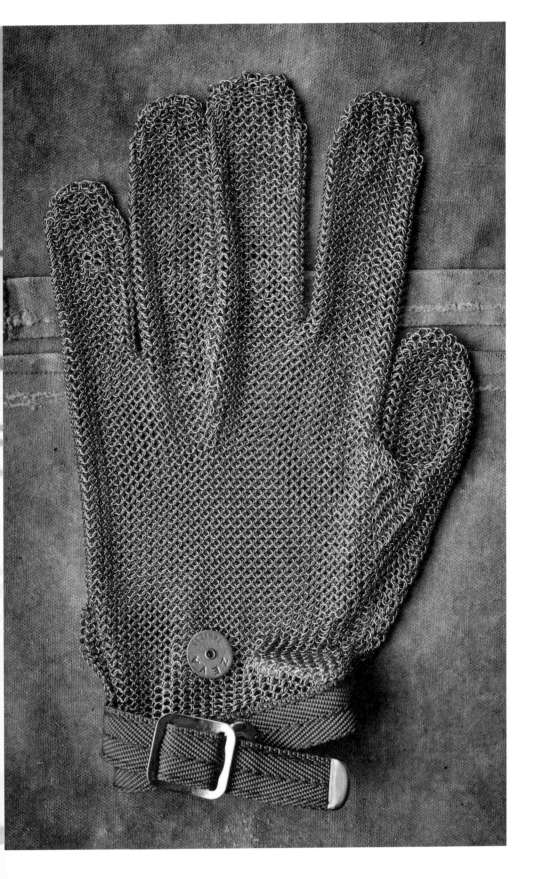

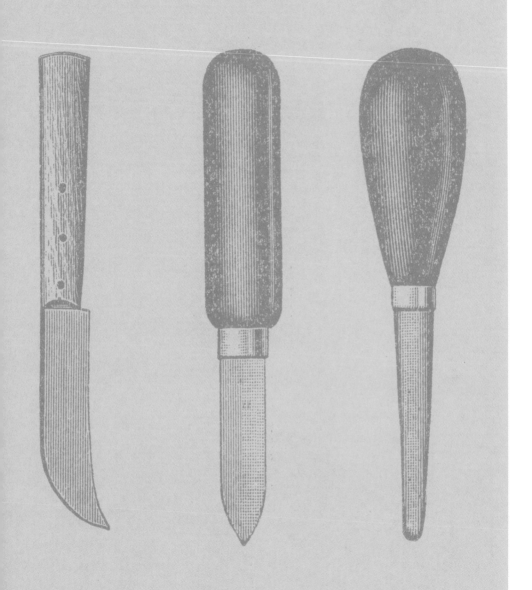

SPECIALISED KNIVES

OYSTER KNIVES

BLADE LENGTH: **63MM**
OVERALL LENGTH: **160MM**
WEIGHT: **35G**
MANUFACTURED BY: **LE ROI DE LA COUPE**
MATERIALS: **STAINLESS STEEL, WOOD, THERMOPLASTIC**
COUNTRY OF ORIGIN: **FRANCE**
USE: **SHUCKING OYSTERS**

UNIQUELY AMONG THE ANIMALS WE EAT, oysters are alive when they come to the table. They survive on land by sealing into themselves a quantity of seawater – kind of a reverse aqualung. Inside the shell they comprise a healthy deposit of (delicious) fat and wiry (delicious) muscle, which they use to keep the shell closed and watertight with the sort of tenacity that us predators can only admire.

With no teeth, claws, venom or ability to breathe fire, oysters are entirely peaceful creatures who, nonetheless, put more humans in hospital every year than the most rampant of raptors. Prising open the shell and nicking the muscle so we can get to the flesh involves such a lethal combination of sharp edge and leverage that most of us who care to tangle with the creatures will have stabbed ourselves in the hand several times.

Oyster knives come in a variety of shapes. One popular style has a short, thick, heart-shaped blade and a substantial circular guard around the hilt, both of which are designed to stop the knife going 'through' the shell and damaging either the oyster flesh or the ball of your thumb. It's a good tool (when combined with a chainmail glove) but lacking in subtlety. Most experienced oyster fanciers and professional shuckers use a thinner knife which, once you've practised on a few dozen, can be slid easily into the right weak spot on the shell perimeter and is sharp enough to sever the muscle easily. You can, as generations of salty sons of the sea have done, do a lovely job with a simple penknife but do be sure it has a locking blade or it will close on your fingers and you'll end up sharing your oysters with a nice doctor at A&E.

This type, common all over France is, as you can see from the photograph, simple in design and quite cheaply made. Even when wielded by experienced hands it will occasionally hit a tough oyster and the end will snap off, so a replacement can't cost too much.

CHEESE KNIVES

....

BLADE LENGTH: **VARIOUS**
OVERALL LENGTH: **VARIOUS**
WEIGHT: **VARIOUS**
MANUFACTURED BY: **ROCKINGHAM FORGE**
(PARMESAN KNIFE **FAMA**)
MATERIALS: **18/10 STAINLESS STEEL, WOOD PRESSURE-TREATED
WITH EPOXY**
COUNTRIES OF ORIGIN: **ENGLAND AND ITALY**
USES: **CUTTING AND SERVING CHEESES**

....

WE ARE STRANGELY CONFLICTED by knives that must be on the table as we dine. Carving knives are kept on the sideboard, sharp knives stay in the kitchen and, with the exception of steak knives (see page 66), we reserve the most inoffensive shapes for the table.

It's easy to see then how the cheese knife evolved. One can imagine a farm worker lopping off a lump of Caerphilly and offering it to a mate on the point of his clasp knife, but such behaviour wouldn't cut it at the more genteel tables. Even elegant table knives with natty little fork arrangements built into the tip specifically for forking could be seen to be, well, maybe just a little 'stabby'. And so we see the development of a politely upswept tip. Nobody could take umbrage at the cheese knife, it even adds a little class, and so we see it gracing tables throughout the gadget-obsessed glory years of the 1950s.

As we become more adventurous in our after-dinner cheese choices though, a problem rears its head – nothing could be less genteel than having to use fingers to prize off a recalcitrant wedge of brie adhering to the blade. Out of this bitter adversity the holey, purpose-designed 'soft cheese knife' is born.

It is now possible to purchase whole sets of 'cheese knives' including items such as this mimsy little chopper, for example, which always come in a lovely box printed with the increasingly tortured rationale behind each different blade shape.

The Parmesan knife, though, is not so lacking in rigour. Tough Parmesan should be cracked into pieces rather than cut, the better to display its gorgeous texture and jewelled distribution of granular salts. This rugged little knife can be jammed into the surface and leverage applied to the knob-like handle until a slab sheers off with a satisfying crack.

ON MENDING AND MODDING

....

ONE OF MY FAVOURITE MOVIE QUOTES comes from the film *Raiders of the Lost Ark*. Explaining his knackered condition to ex-lover Marion Ravenwood, Indy rumbles, 'It's not the years, honey, it's the mileage.'

Like a lot of clapped-out older blokes, I love the idea that, worn with pride, wear and damage equate with character and, like the scars and tattoos on a human body, the repairs and modifications we make to a knife add to its charisma.

Perhaps the simplest modification many chefs make to their knives is to personalise or name them. You can burn an initial into a plastic handle using a heated needle or skewer or mark it with nail polish (see the lovely fading initials of Henry Harris on the handle of the Sabatier on page 46). On older wooden knives, like Nat Gilpin's on page 73 you can easily gouge an identifying mark using another blade. Many knife shops will now engrave a blade with your name, though this somehow doesn't feel quite as rugged and adventurous as Dr Jones.

When knives get damaged they can often be repaired in a way that extends their life and enhances their intrigue. In the picture opposite you'll see a phenolic handle that has cracked and split after a kindly soul put it through a hot cycle in the dishwasher. After the owner had cooled down, he filled the cracks with Fymo (an air-drying modelling compound available from art shops), which, as long as nobody puts it through the dishwasher again, will give years more use.

The beautiful carbon-steel *hankotsu* pictured was carelessly dropped on to a stone floor and the tip snapped off. Half an hour or so with a coarse sharpening stone (see page 202) has reshaped the damaged tip to the owner's specification, making it both useful and pleasingly unique.

Some modifications are less about repair than about making the knife more pleasant to use. Long use of a non-bolstered knife, particularly with wet hands, can cause blisters on the second joint of the forefinger where it hits the back of the blade. This *cai dao* has been wrapped with string for a long shift of fish filleting.

'Sugru' is a silicone-based material that can be moulded by hand and dries to a tough, almost rubber-like finish. Product designers, hackers and geeks love it and it can usually be found 'modding' drones, espresso machines, racing bike gear levers or other hipster gadgets. It was only a matter of time before someone discovered how great it is for creating a high-tech version of the time-honoured string modification.

Repairing or modding a knife is like nursing a much-loved pet through illness or injury. You're delighted to get it back, even if it looks a bit lopsided, and somehow, you love it even more.

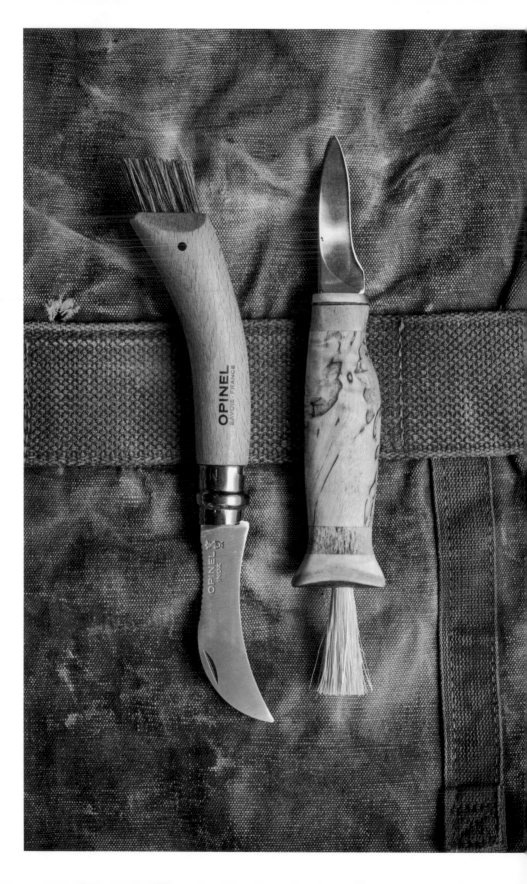

MUSHROOM KNIFE

(OPINEL)
BLADE LENGTH: 70MM
OVERALL LENGTH: 205MM
WEIGHT: 48G
MANUFACTURED BY: OPINEL
MATERIALS: SANDVIK 12C27 STAINLESS STEEL,
OAK, BOAR BRISTLE
COUNTRY OF ORIGIN: FRANCE
USES: HARVESTING AND CLEANING MUSHROOMS

(PUUKKO)
BLADE LENGTH: 56MM
OVERALL LENGTH: 200MM
WEIGHT: 52G
MANUFACTURED BY: N/A (HANDMADE AND UNBRANDED)
MATERIALS: STAINLESS STEEL, ARCTIC CURLY BIRCH,
ANTLER, BRASS, BRISTLE
COUNTRY OF ORIGIN: FINLAND
USES: AS ABOVE

IN THE UK we tend to fear any mushroom that doesn't come hygienically packaged in plastic, however, particularly across Northern Europe, mushroom foraging is a common pastime.

Amid all the choppers, hackers and cleavers, the mushroom knife is a delicate little thing... and so it should be because the mushroom you're harvesting is in fact only the fruiting body of a much larger organism, the mycellium, which remains underground. If the mushroom can be removed with the least possible damage to the underlying mycellium it will go on fruiting regularly for a good long time, improving your harvest, or so the theory goes.

A mushroom knife has a short, sharp blade which is used to cut through the mushroom stem well below the soil surface and a delicate little brush that can remove any adhered dirt without disturbing the spores or damaging the gills. These two examples are (left) the Opinel version, common across France, and (right) a beautiful little model based on the traditional Finnish *puukko* belt knife.

TRUFFLE SLICER

BLADE LENGTH: **58MM**
OVERALL LENGTH: **173MM**
WEIGHT: **98G**
MANUFACTURED BY: **PADERNO**
MATERIALS: **STAINLESS STEEL**
COUNTRY OF ORIGIN: **CANADA**
USES: **SHAVING TRUFFLES, CHOCOLATE, PARMESAN,
GARLIC, BOTTARGA**

TRUFFLES HAVE A UNIQUE TEXTURE that's tougher and woodier than a regular mushroom but softer than a root vegetable. Because their flavour is so strong they need to be served in vanishingly thin flakes or slices and, because the flavour is so evanescent, the slicing must be done at table, barely seconds before eating. The truffle slicer or shaver is elegant enough to place before diners, it is adjustable for thickness, depending on your generosity or greed, and is razor-sharp.

It is sometimes said that a scalloped blade, seen here, is best for black truffles while a straight blade is better for the white variety. I've used this one successfully for both. The straight blades are, though, better for chocolate, Parmesan and garlic – the other things that can be neatly shaved with one of these. Be warned though, this is basically a mandoline – albeit a small one – without any guards. It will, almost certainly, remove exquisitely painful slices of fingertip with equal ease.

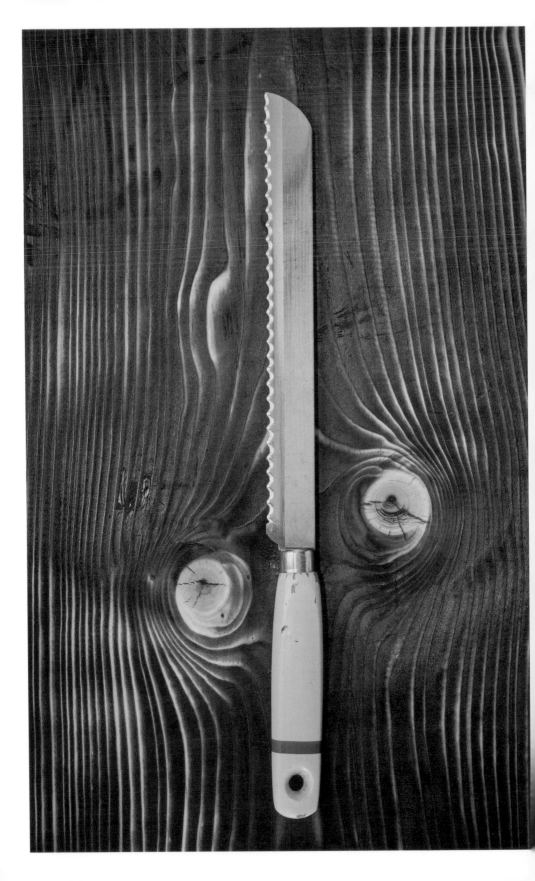

BREAD KNIFE

BLADE LENGTH: **210MM**
OVERALL LENGTH: **310MM**
WEIGHT: **130G**
MANUFACTURED BY: **PRESTIGE (SKYLINE)**
MATERIALS: **STAINLESS STEEL, WOOD,**
CHROME-PLATED STEEL FERULE
COUNTRY OF ORIGIN: **UK**
USE: **SLICING BREAD**

WE BRITISH CANNOT REALLY CLAIM the serrated bread knife entirely as our own but it's not part of the classic French kit and there's no requirement for it in Japanese cuisine, in which wheat is an unusual ingredient and there is no tradition of yeasted breads. The UK was the first nation to industrialise baking and the first to grow to love the large, brick-shaped loaves that benefit from a specialised cutting implement. Fresh bread is difficult to cut neatly, but once it's a day or so old it can usually be sliced with a regular long-bladed knife as long as you're careful and the crust isn't insanely hard. The serrated blade[*], though, means that pretty much anybody can saw a lump off any loaf and those fat, soft, white doorstops have become something of a cultural icon of British cuisine.

Though it's rarely a thing of beauty, the bread knife will be present in British kitchens even when there are no other half-decent knives to speak of – places where the film on the microwave ready-meal is pierced by deranged stabbing with a table knife or possibly scorched with a fag-end. Its existence is a rebuttal of the beauty of good, well-kept knives and yet its functionality and ubiquity give it a sort of ugly charm. Most chefs will tell you that the worst kitchen injuries come from bread knives. In normal use, a plain sharp knife will cut with little force or motion where a bread knife requires a kind of vigorous sawing which can cause far worse damage.[†] Particularly lethal is cutting towards the hand to split a bread roll, causing the 'Beigel Laceration' that's the fifth most common injury in US kitchens.

---

[*] Bread knives with a simple scallop-shaped serration can be sharpened but those with more complex 'saw' edges can't.
[†] There are a few related knives with truly astonishing edge configurations that are sometimes sold as 'freezer' knives – the idea being that something with an edge like a timber saw can be used to cut through solid blocks of frozen material. These are, frankly, horrible objects.

ELECTRIC CARVING KNIFE

....

BLADE LENGTH: **210MM**
OVERALL LENGTH: **498MM**
WEIGHT: **767G**
MANUFACTURED BY: **SEARS ROEBUCK & CO.**
MATERIALS: **STAINLESS STEEL, PLASTIC**
COUNTRY OF ORIGIN: **USA**
USES: **CARVING COOKED MEAT, POULTRY, BAKED GOODS**

....

PATENTS FOR ELECTRIC KNIVES started appearing between the wars amid a blizzard of other 'labour-saving' kitchen gadgetry. They are often billed as 'carving' knives – a term that imbues them with a certain elegant cachet but, in fact, they combine the technology of the serrated bread knife with the electrical hedge trimmer. Two thin blades, loosely clipped together, slide back and forth in a rapid, reciprocating action that will happily chew through most things without requiring too much physical effort.

Electric carving knives are one of the items that, along with the fondue set and the fish knives, were considered suitable wedding presents in the boom years of the 1950s and '60s. As a result many lurk in the back of sideboards, often in their original packaging – a ghostly reminder of a time when social aspiration through consumption once briefly outran utility in design. It's an odd thought, but of all the knives in this book, all the beautiful and costly blades, it is probably this one that holds the most widespread cultural significance. The trust in technology always to improve, the built-in obsolescence, the bounty of the post-war consumer economy, the lure of social aspiration and the power of mass-media advertising... the bizarrely useless* electric carving knife is a fetish to them all.

This American example from Sears Roebuck comes with a wall mount – a popular feature in the new 'fitted' kitchens along with the electric can opener and the kitchen phone. The remarkable colour scheme combines 'avocado' and 'ersatz-teak' to stunning 'contemporary' effect.

---

* Electric carving knives finally found a purpose when prop-, set- and boat-builders discovered that they were superb for cutting the new wonder product, expanded polystyrene foam.

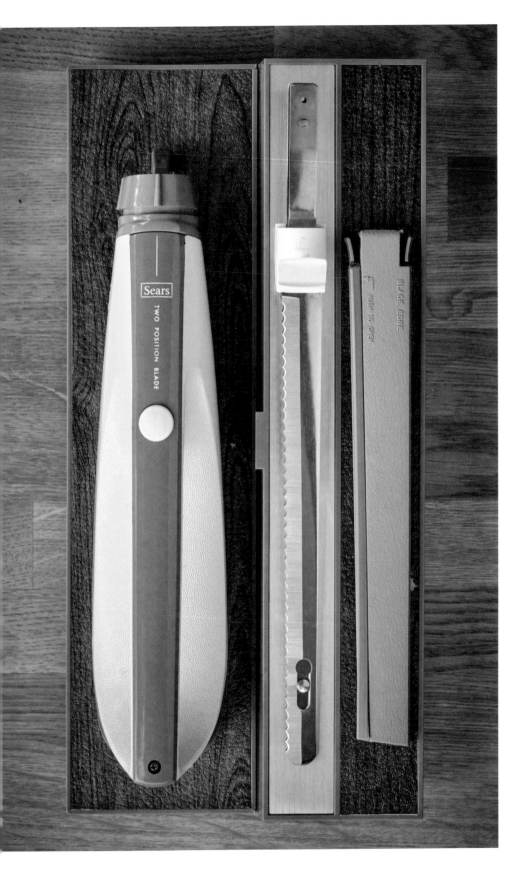

ON CARVING

....

AT THE MEDIEVAL TABLE, large chunks of meat were an extremely high-status food. Cutting them up and distributing the pieces to guests in the correct order of hierarchy was a skilled act. Everyone in the dining hall would have carried their own eating knife at their belt but standing next to the guest of honour, wielding a socking great carving knife was what we would probably refer to today as a 'security risk'. For this reason, the role of the Carver was assigned to a highly trusted and favoured gentleman who would have learned carving as one of the gentlemanly arts.

In 1508 London printer Wynkyn de Worde published the *Boke of Keruynge* or 'Book of Carving', an early self-help book for young men hoping to be accepted at court or into great houses. It covers most of the skills required for organising banquets but also provides a long and much-quoted list of specialist terms for all the ways that different creatures should be carved.*

It's an entertaining list to quote but, sadly, it doesn't actually give us much detail.† Contemporary engravings indicate that the meat may have been brought to the table on the spit on which it was cooked and carved 'vertically'. There is something quite reassuring in the idea that for all his grandeur, Henry VIII was having his meat served to him in exactly the same way you or I might get a doner kebab.

Carving has enormous social significance in many cultures. In *The Seven Pillars of Wisdom*, T.E. Lawrence describes feasting with Howeitat tribesmen in the desert tents and how each man would honour his guests by cutting meat for him from a great brass dish piled high with rice and roast mutton:

---

* dysmembre that heron
   displaye that crane
   disfygure that pecocke
   baioynt that bytture
   batache that cuclewe
   alaye that felande
   wynge that partryche
   wynge that quayle
   niynce that plouer
   thye that pygyon
   border that pauy
   thye that woodcocke
   thye all maner small byrdes

† He does, however, usefully remind the young gentleman that he will gain favour with his master by warming his underwear in front of the fire while helping him dress.

'As the meat pile wore down (nobody really cared about rice: flesh was the luxury) one of the chief Howeitat eating with us would draw his dagger, silver hilted, set with turquoise, a signed masterpiece of Mohammed ibn Zari, of Jauf, and would cut criss-cross from the larger bones long diamonds of meat easily torn up between the fingers; for it was necessarily boiled very tender, since all had to be disposed of with the right hand which alone was honourable.'*

Perhaps the most spectacular carving ritual that's still widely practised today is at a Burns Supper where the great sweating, groaning mass of the haggis is violently stabbed, traditionally with a *sgian dhub* dagger.

Charles Dickens has had a great influence on our national self-image where food is concerned. He used the family meal, the convivial board, as a symbol of plenty, prosperity and general rightness with the world. The *paterfamilias*, clashing knife and steel at the head of a packed table, preparing literally to portion out sustenance and distribute the bounty for which he'd striven, was symbolic of so much of his vision of a healthy, happy society. This image is still part of our cultural DNA to this day and we feel guilty when we grab hurried, packaged meals, rarely, if ever, sitting down together as a family.

There is a particular type of carving set, most commonly found today in junk shops. It comes in a beaten old leather-covered box and comprises a two-tined carving fork, with a sprung, snap-up guard, a steel, so Dad can ritually sharpen the blade, and a 'carving knife'. Usually this has been worn into an irregular spike by Dad's attentions. The handles will be either white bone – intended to mimic ivory – or stag horn, a distant reminder of estates we'll never own. I don't know anyone who still actually uses one of these sets but, whether forgotten wedding presents or left to us by grandparents, they continue to lurk in drawers.

The worn and neglected carving knife is perhaps the sorriest symbol of cultural loss. Dickens' Christmas feasts were works of fiction – wishful thinking, even propaganda – and were probably a lot rarer in reality than we care to imagine; yet we all regret that we no longer assemble for the eating ritual that, in other cultures, is still an important part of family life. Many have forgotten how to carve, some are frightened to try and yet it is a simple thing – to take the food from the oven and, instead of plating it up in the kitchen, bring it to the table and give someone a knife and the honour of having a go.

---

* *Seven Pillars of Wisdom*. Ch. xivi. Available online as part of Project Gutenburg and, without doubt, my all-time-favourite piece of food writing.

The Handy
BOX

STAINLESS
TABLE
CUTLERY

DOES not stain with Food Acids, Vinegar, etc.

AFTER use, simply wash the Blades in HOT Water and dry on a soft cloth in the ordinary way A little washing soda, added to the hot water, will remove any apparent stain.

NO attempt must be made to clean in a Knife Machine or on a board— either will ruin the surface and spoil the appearance of the knife.

SHARPEN occasionally on a Steel.

DO not put the Handles in the HOT Water.

Manufactured in
SHEFFIELD,
ENGLAND.

10 RULES OF CARVING

....

1

REST THE MEAT before carving. There are several guidelines for this: one-third of the cooking time; 10 minutes per 3 centimetres of thickness; 20 minutes per kilogram, but the best way is to use a probe thermometer. Once the core temperature of the meat has dropped to 50°C the muscle fibres will have relaxed fully, meaning that juices will stay inside the meat instead of pumping out all over the serving plate. Properly rested meat slices beautifully, even across the grain, without breaking up.

2

CHECK THAT YOUR KNIFE IS SHARP. Use the longest carving knife you have to make long-stroke cuts. Take it slowly. If the knife is sharp enough you might even consider placing your finger along the spine to better control the blade.

3

YEAH, SURE, we'd all like to be able to take off wafer thin, regular thickness slices like the bloke at the carvery, but he does it all day and probably has some boringly homogenous, slightly overcooked meat to work with. Don't sweat it. There is absolutely no shame in carving the kind of slices you feel comfortable cutting and that you enjoy eating. In my case, that's thick and juicy.

4

USE A CARVING FORK to hold the joint steady but always slice either parallel to the tines or away from them. There are few feelings as unpleasant as sawing through the joint and running your carefully sharpened blade into the fork. Pros also use the fork to apply tension to poultry legs and wings while carving. Put the end of the leg between the tines and twist the fork. This should pull the leg away from the body and make it obvious where to slip in the knife.

5

CARVING BIRDS is a lot easier if the wishbone has been removed before cooking. This gives a straight, uninterrupted slice through the breast.

6

WITH CHICKENS and turkeys, it's also worth locating the hip joints from inside the cavity and nicking through the tendons with a sharp knife before cooking.

7

WHEN YOU'RE READY TO CARVE, take off both legs with simple vertical cuts through the hip joint. Remove the breasts whole, though try, if you can, to leave a healthy chunk of meat at the base of the wing. This makes the wing a good serving by itself. The breast can be cut into slices across the grain. Use the heel of the knife to go through the 'knee'. Take it carefully and just let the knife find its own way through the joint. The drumstick is a single serving, the thigh meat can be cut away from the bone in long slices.

8

CARVE A LEG OF LAMB or venison by holding the bone, wrapped in cloth, in one hand, raising it up from the board and cutting in long strokes, parallel to the bone and away from your body. This looks immensely impressive and is as close as you're going to get to being Wynkyn de Worde's young nobleman.

9

CUT THE MEAT AWAY from beef ribs first, so you have a single boneless piece before you start to slice it across the grain. Separate the ribs later and offer them for gnawing purposes.

10

WITH BEEF, LAMB OR PORK, only slice as much as you want to serve so the meat stays hot and leftovers can be stored as a single piece. Poultry should be completely removed from the bone as soon as possible as chilling it on the carcass gives an unpleasant, fowly taste.

AXE

BLADE LENGTH: **65MM**
OVERALL LENGTH: **320MM**
WEIGHT: **677G**
MANUFACTURED BY: **WETTERLINGS MANUFAKTUR AB**
MATERIALS: **CARBON STEEL, HICKORY**
COUNTRY OF ORIGIN: **SWEDEN**
USES: **SPLITTING WOOD FOR OUTDOOR COOKING, LIGHT BUTCHERY AND SLAUGHTER**

SO MANY DIFFERENT COOKING KNIVES can be used in a similar way to the axe that it would perhaps be wrong not to consider the original as a culinary implement. American butchers sometimes refer to the cleaver as a 'meat axe' and I have seen several Scandinavian barbecue teams use the same axes they use to dress logs to cut up and serve the sheep they've been roasting.

The axe in the picture is a small Wetterlings Hunter's Hatchet #115. It's light and is designed to be worn at the belt. We are told by its makers: 'A sharp Hatchet gives you the extra power needed at slaughter – as well as that knife. This is also a definite item to be keeping in the back of your vehicle when the unexpected happens. You can handle a tree on the road as well as injured animals needing to be taken care of.'

I've ground mine perhaps just a little sharper than for wood splitting and use it whenever I roast large pieces of meat over open fires for parties.

PICNIC KNIVES

YOU CAN, OF COURSE, SURVIVE ALFRESCO EATING by carefully packing whatever knives you'd usually have used in the kitchen, but quite a lot of ingenuity has been poured into designing knives specially for picnicking, and quite a few traditional countryman's knives, from various traditions, have become popular fixtures in the hamper.

On the left-hand side in the photograph is a 'Bâtard Folding Picnic Knife' from Lamson and Goodnow in the US. It works well for bread cutting – though I personally favour tearing – and the serrated edge can also be turned to carving cooked meat.

Laguiole, like Sabatier, is actually not a trademark name but an indicator of a style of knife made in the French city of Thiers. They can vary massively in quality. The second knife from the left is an elderly Laguiole that's particularly useful for outdoor grilling. The extra-long blade means that it has to be stored in a purpose-built sheath, but it unfolds into a creditable, though rusty, carving knife.

Next along is the high-quality, traditionally shaped Laguiole which I keep in the glove compartment of the car for culinary emergencies on the road. Next to that, a chunkier clasp knife, also in Laguiole style, which is good for cheese that puts up a fight. On the right is a Spanish blade with an olivewood handle. It bears no maker's name but can make extremely short work of the hardest chorizo.

At the bottom is an obscenely expensive folding knife and fork set from French cutler, Claude Dozorme. It's a beautiful thing but I can't help feeling that if you need a knife and fork, you should probably be eating indoors.

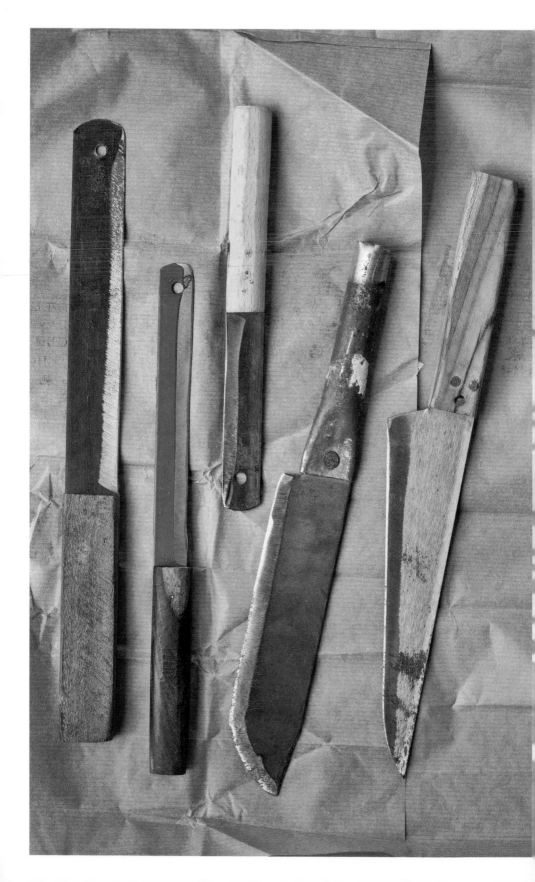

INDIAN MARKET KNIVES

OVERALL LENGTH: **VARIOUS**
MANUFACTURED BY: **HANDMADE**
MATERIALS: **WASTE AND BROKEN SAW BLADES, AUTOMOTIVE
LEAF SPRINGS, SCRAP PIPE AND WOOD FROM PACKING CASES
AND PALLETS**
COUNTRY OF ORIGIN: **INDIA**
USES: **ALL PURPOSES**

THIS BUNDLE OF KNIVES was picked up in a street market in Jodhpur for 2,000 rupees from the elderly woman who manufactured them, but they might easily have come from a market almost anywhere on the planet. Anywhere there are factories or garages, tool steel is recycled daily. The blades on the left are made from broken hacksaw blades or the leaf springs from scrap cars. They've been sharpened either on a stone or a rudimentary sharpening wheel and the blades are 'riveted' to the handle with nails or wire.

India doesn't have a distinctive, indigenous culinary knife, so it's interesting how these – like French or Japanese knives – have evolved out of grips and cutting actions. The pointy knife on the right can obviously make long slicing actions like a *yanagiba* and has enough knuckle clearance to be held in a 'hammer' grip. The second knife is a chopper in the traditions of the *usuba* or the *cai dao*. The remaining three, with no knuckle clearance and round handles, are designed to be used off the board in the 'cutting-towards-the-thumb' style.

DAO BAO

BLADE LENGTH: **116MM**
OVERALL LENGTH: **225MM**
WEIGHT: **47G**
MANUFACTURED BY: **HANDMADE**
MATERIALS: **SCRAP SAW BLADE, LOCAL WOOD, BRASS**
COUNTRY OF ORIGIN: **THAILAND**
USES: **PEELING AND SHREDDING HARD VEGETABLES
AND FRUIT AT ROADSIDES OR STALLS**

THE DAO BAO is a vegetable paring knife from South-East Asia and a perfect example of a global family of knives with a 'guarded' blade that controls how deep it can penetrate. In one sense this is the mechanism of a spiralizer or mandoline, mounted on a handle.

Passing the knife along the surface of a hard vegetable produces a long ribbon of material – just like a simpler version of Japanese *katsuramuki* rotary cutting (see page 98) – which makes it ideal for reducing a challenging root into something that's pleasantly palatable as a salad. It also, of course, makes it an ideal tool for fast, accurate peeling. In fact, the *dao bao* is a direct relative of your mum's old-school potato peeler or even the commercial 'speed peeler' beloved of pro chefs.

The *dao bao*, unlike other knives, is also influenced by the posture adopted while using it. It's popular with street traders who may well prepare food outdoors, in a squatting position, paring veg straight on to a plate or into a pot.

This *dao bao* has a second blade along one edge which can be used for more regular chopping on a board.

FRUIT AND VEG
CARVING KNIVES

....

KEENLY PRICED AT UNDER £40 ON EBAY, this Chinese-made fruit and veg carving outfit might be the cheapest set of knives you can get that you didn't know you need.

Across China, Japan and South-East Asia, vegetable carving is part of an elegant table setting and chefs take the opportunity to display incredible creativity in biomass-based flights of fancy that echo the great *pièces montées* of Antonin Carême.

You can do some pretty neat work with a small paring knife and a scalpel but this kit also contains dozens of tiny chisels, gouges, whittlers and turners, along with templates and cutters appropriate to a variety of Chinese social occasions.

Buy a kit and experiment. If you use potatoes you can always boil and mash your failures. You may never use 75 per cent of the tools in the box, even if you can work out how you're supposed to, but you'll find dozens of ways to use the rest.

A good example of this is the melon baller, that odd chrome job in the middle of the case with two hemispherical spoon ends. On the face of it this is the most fatuous of tools, almost the definition of pointlessly mimsy kitchen gadget. After all, who balls melons, these days... who ever did? And yet, in most classically trained cooks' knife rolls you'll find one or two, squirrelled away. Like tiny ice-cream scoops with sharpened edges, though they may have originally been intended to make decorative fruit spheres, they make themselves useful in dozens of ways in the professional kitchen; removing pips and pulp from tomatoes, stripping the seeds from halved cucumbers, neatly deseeding melons, scraping the pith from citrus peel and removing the eyes from potatoes and even, we are told, pigs' heads.

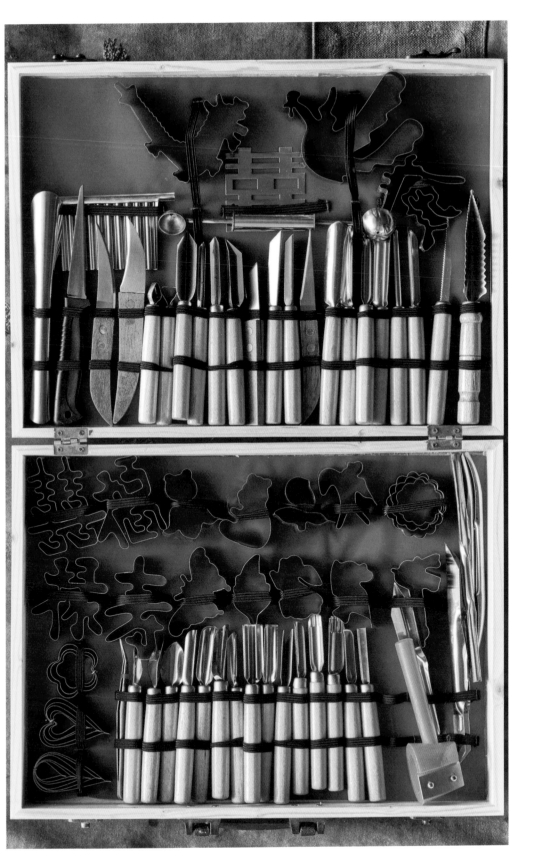

JAMONERO/SALMON SLICER

BLADE LENGTH: **320MM**
OVERALL LENGTH: **435MM**
WEIGHT: **141G**
MANUFACTURED BY: **GLOBAL**
MATERIALS: **CROMOVA18 STAINLESS STEEL**
COUNTRY OF ORIGIN: **JAPAN**
USE: **DISPLAY CARVING**

THIS MODERN SLICER is made by Global, one of the first Japanese companies to export knives to the West. Fine *jamón ibérico* on the bone and Scottish smoked wild salmon are both high-status foods that demand careful slicing as close as possible to the time of serving as well as a certain amount of tableside theatre; the long, thin, wickedly sword-like slicer is just the tool for the job.

Like the sashimi cutting blades, the slicer is long, allowing a slice to be taken with a single stroke and avoiding unpleasant 'sawing' marks on the cut surface of the food.

The blade is flexible so it can be bent flat against the inside of the salmon skin at the end of the stroke. Because the blade runs parallel to skin and bone, it need never touch them, or indeed, the cutting board. A slicer, therefore, if used carefully, can be given a much more acute and ultimately sharp grind than other knives because it's never going to be traumatised by hard stuff.

MANDOLINE

BLADE LENGTH: **100MM**
OVERALL LENGTH: **390MM**
WEIGHT: **1600G**
MANUFACTURED BY: **BRON-COUKE**
MATERIALS: **STAINLESS STEEL**
COUNTRY OF ORIGIN: **FRANCE**
USES: **FINE SLICING AND SHREDDING OF
VEGETABLES, FRUIT, CHEESE**

FEW CUTTING DEVICES cause such terror in the kitchen as the mandoline. It should be a lovely thing – a captive knife blade, safely fixed in a protective frame, over which food is slid. The blade is covered and its depth is adjustable, much like an upturned wood plane. It should be a safer way to cut than a big, ugly naked knife. In truth, the mandoline is so open to misuse that almost everyone who's ever used one has cut themselves in a memorably unpleasant way.

Used with care and with a guard, a mandoline can make immaculately thin slices of vegetable that would shame even the most adept commis chef. It can also be used to cut a corrugated 'wavy' edge, and a range of vertical 'comb' blades can be switched which, at a single pass, turn the slices into fine julienne.

The traditional French model* is a heavy, beautifully engineered piece of chrome-plated kitchen sculpture. It's also a bear to clean.

---

* I've always kept my French mandoline in its original, bloodstained box. It reminds me to use the guard every time.

JAPANESE MANDOLINES

....

BLADE LENGTH: **90MM**
OVERALL LENGTH: **310MM**
WEIGHT: **259G**
MANUFACTURED BY: **BENRINER**
MATERIALS: **STAINLESS STEEL, PLASTIC**
COUNTRY OF ORIGIN: **TAIWAN**
USES: **FINE SLICING AND SHREDDING OF VEGETABLES**

....

KATSURAMUKI is a knife technique unique to Japanese cuisine.* It's fiendishly difficult, however, and those super-thin slices and shreds are still required even in home cooking, so a mandoline is exactly the right tool. Not the big, intimidating chrome number, beloved of the French, but a light, plastic, domestic version that does the whole job just as well, just as fast and costs only pennies. These are so efficient that many western chefs now use them in place of a traditional mandoline.

Perhaps because even a plastic mandoline cuts fingers, the Japanese have also come up with the 'turning slicer' in which the vegetable is mounted on a rotating axle and then offered up to a fixed blade. The original type (below) holds the veg vertically and cuts the face, but there are other versions where the vegetable rotates horizontally while the blade is applied to the side – more accurately replicating katsuramuki but only useable on daikon and a few other cylindrical veg.

Turning slicers were briefly discovered by the 'healthy eating' crowd and re-marketed as expensive 'spiralizers'. In these more enlightened times you should be able to pick one up for next to nothing.

---

* See description on page 98.

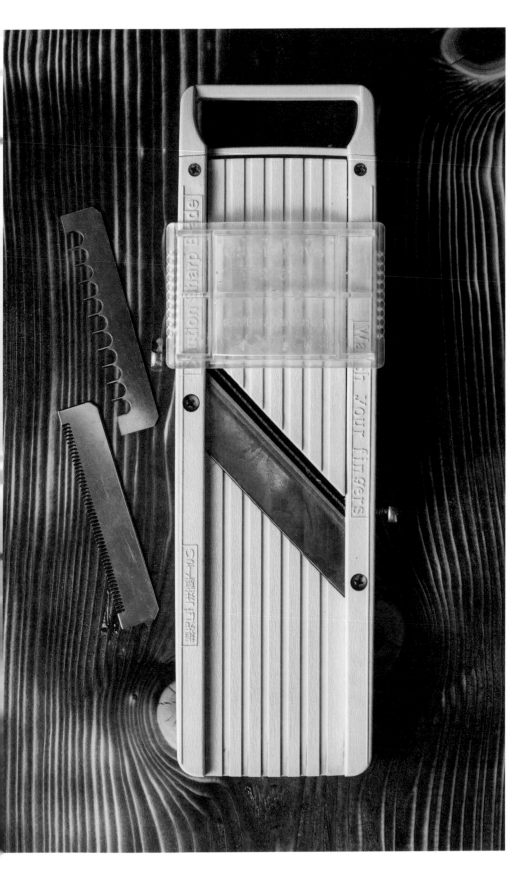

MEZZALUNA

BLADE LENGTH: **286MM**
OVERALL LENGTH: **286MM**
WEIGHT: **260G**
MANUFACTURED BY: **A.L.O.**
MATERIALS: **CARBON STEEL, OLIVEWOOD**
COUNTRY OF ORIGIN: **UNKNOWN**
USES: **FINE CHOPPING OF MEAT, HERBS, NUTS**

MEZZALUNA MEANS 'HALF MOON', the Italian name for a two-handled semi-circular knife with a rocking action. Small mezzalunas* are usually reserved for chopping nuts, herbs and garlic and can have one, two or occasionally three parallel blades. There is also a version with a single handle, mounted in the middle of the blade that comes with a special dished wooden chopping bowl – sometimes called a 'hachinette'. In this incarnation they fit into the nice-but-pointless class of kitchen gadgetry as they offer no advantage in terms of function or efficiency over a regular knife and are a complete pain to clean and store.

Larger mezzalunas though, single-bladed, substantial and sharp, can be used to mince meat. The French, in fact, call them 'hachoirs' and, because they operate with a downwards slicing action instead of the forced mashing and extrusion of the mincing machine, they produce a coarser mince with cuboid chunks that retain more juice. A *hachoir* will produce better steak tartare and far juicier burgers than any other tool or appliance.

* *Berceuses* in French.

SHARPNESS

ON BEING CUT

....

EVERY ONE OF US WHO USES A KNIFE WILL, at some point, have cut themselves. To call it an 'accident' seems foolish because we know it's going to happen. Amateurs cut themselves because they don't have enough skill but professionals cut themselves just as much because the skills they have learned mean using the knife faster and more often. There are acts of stupidity to be avoided – cutting food that's improperly held, trying to catch a falling blade, using the knife for a purpose it was never intended, leaving a blade in the wrong place. It might even be possible to avoid getting cut altogether by buying in more pre-cut ingredients, or perhaps using food preparation gadgets and machines, laden with safety guards, cut-outs and plastered with warning notices. There are perfectly serviceable cut-proof gloves, but most cooks would rather die the Death of a Thousand Cuts than go down that route. It would detach them, they'd say, from a tactile relationship with the food.

Cuts, then, 'go with the territory'.

We are only cooks; when you cut us, do we not bleed? Like everyone else we feel the initial, almost acid burn of the blade passing through skin laden with nerve endings. But then something entirely different sets in. When you ask cooks about their cuts, it's never the pain they recall. They'll talk about the blood. These days, when chefs get drunk, they often whip out their phones to show pictures of the latest gory flap of skin hidden under a blue plaster.* Or they'll talk about how they dealt with it and got straight back to work.

The level of machismo involved can be foolish. In the heat of service, cooks will wrap a wound in cling film or a rubber glove and keep going – often, thereby, missing the vital time window in which a serious cut can still be viably stitched. Insane resilience in the face of an injury that would floor a civilian is one of the many unhealthy behavioural traits by which chefs continue to define themselves.† Chefs often speak of cauterising a cut on the hotplate and continuing to work.‡

From outside the professional kitchen, this kind of behaviour looks absurd. It is counterintuitive to worsen a wound rather than immediately ameliorating it, and yet,

---

* Blue, or 'disclosing' plasters are used in kitchens so they can be easily spotted if they drop off into food. In large factories they also have metal tape woven through them, like the strip in a banknote, so they can be picked up by metal detectors.

† In *Down and Out in Paris and London*, George Orwell is famously baffled by the kitchen obsession with physical 'hardness', with being, as the slang of the time had it, 'débrouillard'.

‡ I used to believe this was a myth but I've now seen it happen enough times to know it's horribly true.

as we build relationships with our own knives, even those of us who cook for fun rather than a profession begin to change our attitude.

A key part of learning to sharpen a knife is testing the edge. In the beginning you cut newspaper to check that you've got a good edge but pretty soon you find yourself doing what the pros do, placing your thumb on the spine of the knife and feeling the edge with the balls of three fingers. Initially, it's terrifying. Most of your mental faculties, for very sensible reasons, are working to make you withdraw your body from the threat. Yet the feeling of control as you test the razor edge – just catching in the cornified outer layers of skin, never penetrating, the microscopic irregularities scratching against the loops and whorls of your fingerprint – is that of almost literally 'dancing on the edge'.

Even now, as you read this, I'm prepared to bet that you're looking at the scars on your own hands. Fading traces of thin white lines, a knotty little cicatrice where a slipped knife caught the nail. Oddly I'm looking at a place on my left hand where I once suffered a monstrous slash – a proper A&E job – and I realise it's healed without trace. I feel robbed. All that mess and nothing to show for it.

To own, love and properly use a knife is to feel that you've overcome your fear of it, learned to master it, yet it has lost none of its potency in the transaction. The cut becomes a symbol of the delicate line you've walked. For all the times you have taken your knife in your hand and it worked for you beautifully it is still capable of turning on you. In other parts of our lives we usually correct, avoid or dispose of things that hurt us but in this sense our relationship with the knife is like the one we have with a particularly favoured or thoroughbred pet. It's okay if it occasionally bites or kicks. It shows spirit... it's how it is.

HOW TO SHARPEN

....

PUTTING THE CUTTING EDGE on to the blade is a two-stage process of abrading (to create the edge) and aligning. You could call these processes, with pleasing rhyme, 'stoning and honing'.

To make an edge on a blade where there currently isn't one, a little metal must be removed from each side. It must be ground into a wedge. This can be done with all sorts of abrasive materials like the carborundum belts on a linisher, a wheel or block made with diamond dust or the more delicate 'water stone'. The important thing is that the material is harder than the steel of the blade and has a rough enough surface to cut.

Water stones can be naturally occuring rock, cut into flat panels or a ceramic equivalent. The important thing about them is that they have a plane surface, can be soaked in water to keep them cool during grinding and are available in a variety of grades of roughness.

The blade is ground with the abrasive on alternate sides, creating two flat planes at an acute angle to each other which eventually meet. As the edge gets thinner it also becomes weaker, so at the point when it is actually 'sharp', the kinetic forces of grinding will naturally bend the edge over to one side. This makes what's called a 'burr': an edge that you can feel on one side or other of the blade. This is the point at which to stop the abrasive process. You've taken away as much metal as you need. If you continue grinding, you push the burr back in the opposite direction, creating a line of weakness and a thinner point just behind the edge. This is called a 'wire edge'. The wire edge will snap off and leave a honeable edge behind – you sometimes see it when cleaning a blade during sharpening – but strictly it is removing more metal than you need to.

Now the edge must be aligned or honed. This means rubbing the edge against a surface that gently pushes it, from both sides, until it is precisely in line with the blade. Honing materials can vary. In the food world, blades are traditionally honed with a steel, a plain metal rod in a handle, while barbers and, oddly enough, surgeons have traditionally honed their ferociously sharp blades on leather 'strops'. I know one good butcher who hones his knife on the metal edge of his butcher block and one knife collector who hones his on the pages of *Vogue*. Glossy magazine paper – coated with a gypsum-like material and rolled under pressure to give it that superb finish for ink – makes a surprisingly excellent material for ultra-fine honing and polishing.*

---

*   ... which is why, after much consideration, this book is printed on uncoated stock – we didn't want you misusing it.

SHAPING THE EDGE

BURR

MATERIAL
REMOVED

ABRASION

BLUNT BLADE

SHARP BLADE

It is important to understand the difference between 'stoning and honing', abrading and aligning, because different sharpening systems can do both to some degree. Coarse water stones, for example, strip metal off a knife edge at a terrific rate, making that 'wedge' with great efficiency, but the finest grades have so little abrasive quality that they merely 'polish', taking away almost nothing but helping to align the edge. A traditional metal 'steel' has no abrasive qualities at all and is merely there to align the edge where a more modern 'diamond steel' – coated with a fine dust of industrial diamond abrasive – can wear a knife away as fast as a wheel. Even strops can be plain leather, with no abrasive, or dressed with a 'compound' that's a very fine abrasive.

Sharpening well, by hand, is actually a lot simpler than is usually assumed. It's a forgiving process which will almost certainly result in a better cutting edge no matter what you do... but it does depend to some degree on your ability to present the blade to the work surface at a reasonably consistent angle. This makes people nervous. Proprietary knife-sharpeners take away that worry by fixing the sharpening medium at the correct angle and guiding the blade through. Expensive ones have two wheels spun by an electric motor and some use two mini-'steels', set in a v-shape with a guide to hold the knife in the right position.

For serious blade geeks in other, less benign, areas of knife worship, there are very expensive sharpening jigs which clamp the knife in position and then allow you to sweep a selection of small, flat waterstones along the blade with a long pivoting arm. These I feel are vital for creating the kind of visually perfect edge that matters to collectors but may be a bit much if you're mainly about getting faster at reducing onions to dice.

A knife-sharpener, if you're prepared to stump up a few quid, is no bad thing. I often recommend the Japanese ones to friends who don't necessarily have the time or the inclination to hand-sharpen. They guarantee a great, working result for almost no effort and immeasurably enhance the experience of cooking. They do, though, work by abrasion, which means they chew through your knives at speed.

Here's the thing though – and I'm probably oversharing here – but being alone in the kitchen, after everyone's tucked up in bed, with something nice on the radio and my knife roll and stones... Well, it's contemplative, meditative, calming. Taking each knife out of its place, remembering how it performed last time, correcting it gently, improving it, caring for it and getting it ready to work again – it's just lovely. The time and effort you spend maintaining your knives is the thing that distinguishes them from all other tools. A set of sockets is as dumb as a bag of spanners: a roll of knives is something that has as much in it as you're prepared to give. Sharpening your knives, in the end, is what it's all about.

STONE

Since the first metal knives were made they've been sharpened on stones. You can still pick up a smooth pebble and use it to align your blade but the best naturally occurring sharpening stones are those with hard abrasive particles – or 'grit' – in a softer matrix. As the grit abrades the metal the stone itself is worn away, making a constantly renewed, flat abrasive surface.

Natural stone whetstones are quarried in various parts of the world and are beautiful things, but obviously there is very little consistency in the size of grit. Man-made stones – made of carefully graded abrasive grit and bound in a resin or ceramic matrix – are therefore more commonly used.

Japanese knives are sharpened using three stones, the *arato*, *nakato* and *shiageto* (coarse, medium and finishing, respectively). A fourth type, the *nagura*, is used to flatten the medium and finishing stones and create a polishing slurry on the surface. Lubricants are necessary on most sharpening stones and good edges are made on tools with carborundum stones and oil. Japanese stones, though, would clog with oil so they are soaked in water before use and the cutting surface is splashed with it while working. This is why Japanese stones are called 'water stones'.

GRITS

120–500	Very coarse grit. Only for grinding an edge on a knife blank or serious reshaping
500–2000	Coarse grit for initial grind and removing small chips and irregularities
2000–6000	Medium grit to remove scratches and refine edge
6000–10000	Fine grit to polish and hone

Stones come in different shapes and sizes and some as 'combinations' with blocks of two different grits bonded back to back. Good brands to look out for are King (Ice Bear or Sun Tiger), CERAX, Shapton and Naniwa.

With water and grit splashing about, sharpening can be a messy business. You can hold your stone steady on a folded cloth but a stone clamp will enable you to work over the top of a tray of water – a convenient and cleaner option.

Stones should be kept clean and dry between sessions, either in their original boxes or in plastic or wood cases.

MADE IN JAPAN

刃の黒幕

▲SHAPTON®
CERAMIC
WHETSTONE

K0710
MELON-SUPER

MADE IN JAPAN

KING PARTE #800

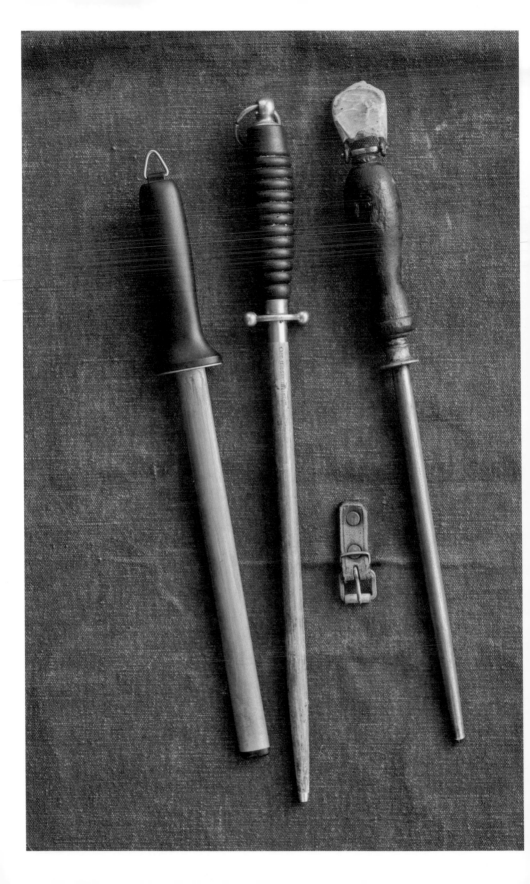

STEEL

There's nothing TV producers like more than their celebrity chef staring down the camera while nonchalantly 'sharpening' his huge knife on a hone or steel. It's a wonderfully powerful image, and I'm sure there are therapists who could make a lot of money out of analysing the behaviour, but in truth I bet the chef won't be doing it with his favourite knife. Regular steeling to realign the blade is important when you're working with the knife all day but it's not something you can do without a degree of concentration and care. The steel is harder than the blade and banging them together in a showy, noisy display will cause irreparable harm, no matter how good it looks.

Any bar of good, hard steel can be used to hone the blade – in some butcher's you'll see them doing it on the metal binding brackets at the corner of the chopping block. But the traditional rod shape in a handle is convenient and, particularly for high volume meat and fish processors, means that it can be worn at the belt in a holster or on a hook, easily to hand.

Though a smooth finish does the job well, many steels are supplied with longitudinal ribbing. Depending on how hard your knife is this may actually have an abrasive effect and remove some material.

More popular today is the 'diamond' steel, often with a flatter, oval profile and coated with a ferocious abrasive material. These things could probably put a working edge on a length of railway line in just a few inept strokes – they do so by tearing away huge amounts of metal. Although a tremendous boon in the commercial environment, where unskilled people can keep lethal edges on cheap knives, if you have a knife you care about I'd honestly rather watch you put it through the dishwasher than go at it with one of these.

STROP

The word 'strop' comes from the same etymological root as 'strap' and it is usually precisely that: a leather strap or belt, hanging from something solid at one end, against which you can rub your blade, the hard surface of the leather gently pushing the blade edge into perfect alignment. You'll have seen barbers doing it with razors. That kind of 'flip-flop' action on the tight, stretched leather seems to work perfectly for the short, straight edge of a razor but it can be a bit more challenging to carry off with a full-size kitchen knife. Flat 'bench' strops comprise a bigger piece of leather, glued to a board, usually with some sort of handle to hold them steady while working.

A new strop is just naked, untreated hide but many people like to 'dress' it with a polishing compound, basically a very, very fine abrasive in a waxy base that is rubbed on to the leather like polish. There are several grades of polishing compound available but for the very finest results you can use 'jeweller's rouge' (a mildly abrasive automotive polish like Autosol available online) or – the secret weapon of several knifemakers – cheap toothpaste.

Personally, I reckon the blade should be sharp and polished enough that I don't want any further abrasive involved in what is always the last stage in the process. As most flat strops are double-sided though, it might be a good compromise to dress one side.

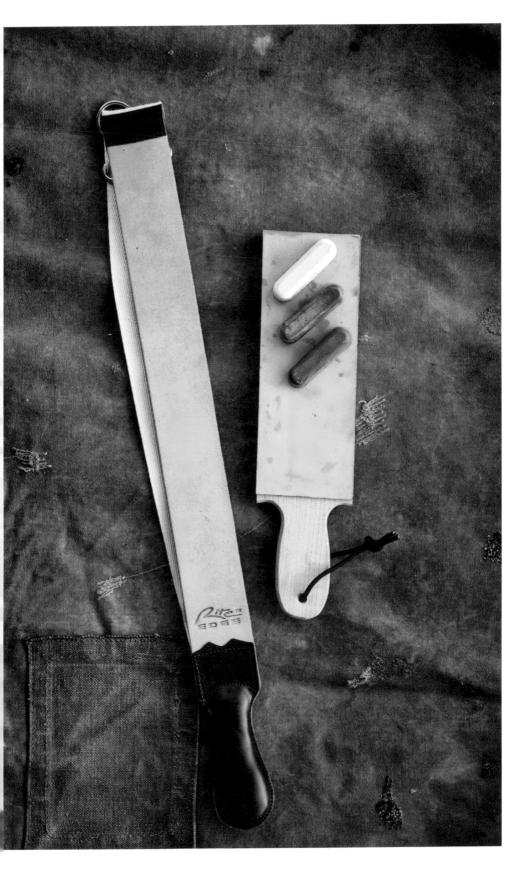

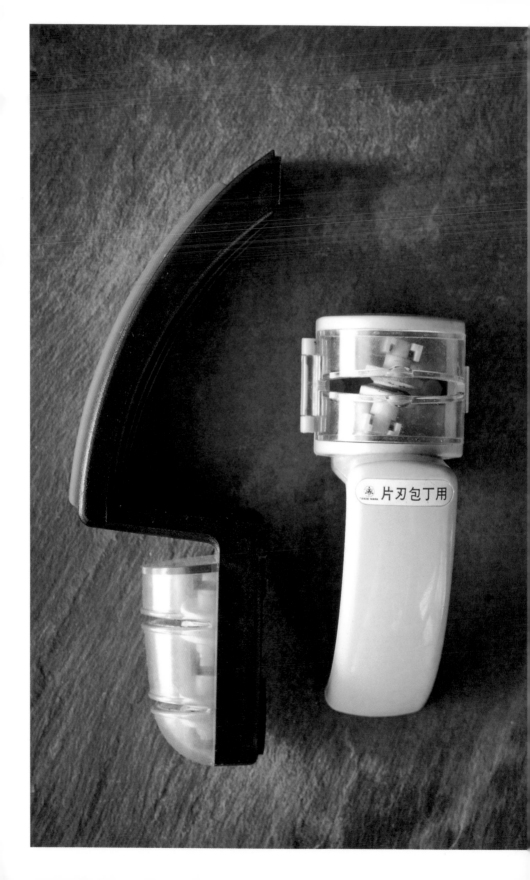

WHEEL

Much human ingenuity has been expended on the foolproof domestic knife-sharpener with varying degrees of success. In principle it should be simple to arrange a sharpening medium at a precise angle and in such a way that even the most harried home cook could drag the knife through it and put on a good edge. Many have tried and many have failed – probably because such an arrangement would only work with a knife that was otherwise well looked after. A sharpener works well for the first few months but, once you've used your knife as a can-opener, snapped off the tip and pressed it into service as a screwdriver, no amount of dragging it through a gadget is going to rebuild it.

But, even to a true devotee of the stones and the strop, there is remarkable convenience in a knife-sharpener. Something you can turn to to quickly correct an edge when you haven't time for the full, delightful ritual.

Japanese water stone sharpeners have two small wheels, made of the correct grade of stone, between which the blade is pulled. They are cleverly arranged so the sides of each wheel create the correct grind angle and the motion of the blade gently rotates them to provide a constantly renewing sharpening surface.* There is also a small water reservoir below to keep the stones both wet and clean.

I will be honest here. A good water stone, wheel-type sharpener, used carefully and with the wheels regularly replaced with fresh ones, will make a beautiful edge on a knife. Depending on your skills, possibly as good as you'll get with bench stones. The only thing they lack is the requisite sense of ritual. Sure... you don't have to drag the whole sharpening kit out of the cupboard and spend half an hour honouring and polishing your favourite blade but, well... isn't that the whole point?

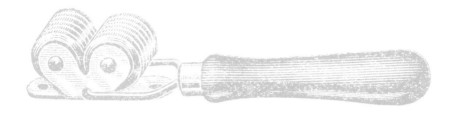

---

* If you have a single-ground knife, you can buy a wheel set with a slightly different angle and with one polishing rather than sharpening wheel. These also work very well but it's obviously vital to pull the knife in the same direction over the wheels every time.

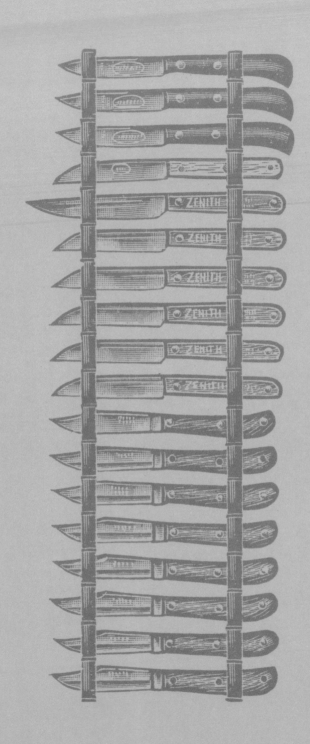

KNIFE ACCESSORIES

KNIFE ROLL

THE TRADITIONAL CHEF'S KNIFE ROLL was a thick, white canvas affair with pockets for the handle-end of the knives. This provided no real protection against the blades knocking into each other but, as they'd easily cut through any canvas pocket they were thrust into, there was no really sensible way to reverse the knives. Many chefs would interlace a kitchen cloth or towel between the blades to keep them apart when the roll was closed but this did nothing to protect anyone if they dropped the roll or picked it up incorrectly. The traditional roll worked well if the knives were mainly being stored in a drawer or locker and if the whole thing was fitted into a metal toolbox when being carried for any distance.

Today, knife rolls are available in all kinds of materials, from the original heavy canvas to Cordura ballistic nylon and even wonderfully flashy models in leather. When choosing a knife roll consider two things above all: firstly, safety from cutting yourself while carrying knives or when removing one for use; secondly, protecting the blades from damaging each other.

Plastic or magnetic blade guards that clip on to each blade can help, as can velcro restraints inside the roll and, in some cases, a heavy sheepskin lining.

KNIFE RACK

....

THERE IS ONE, slightly obsessive, piece of workshop practice that I'm proud to have inherited from my grandfather. Ron believed that any tool that wasn't either in your hand or in its designated storage space was an accident waiting to happen. It's a good system – so good, in fact, that it's standard practice in places like operating theatres and Formula One pit areas. When the patient has been closed up or the car is back on the track and doing 200mph, that's precisely the wrong time to notice that one of your tools is missing. In the same way, the worst time to notice that your *yanagiba* has gone missing is when your mother-in-law has 'popped it in the sink for a nice wash' and the suds are going that ominous carmine colour.

This is why I love magnetic knife racks. Sure, they look great – keeping all your lovely knives on permanent display, not damaging each other in a drawer – but I also look at that rack often when I'm working in the kitchen and if a blade is missing, and it's not in my hand, I know it's waiting to cause trouble and I can stop and hunt it down.

Magnetic strips are available cheaply from kitchen supply houses and their only disadvantage is that they can scratch the backs of your blades. There are terrifically expensive racks with powerful magnets channelled into the back of gorgeous pieces of wood which overcome this problem, but I prefer the tip I was given by James Morton, baker/brewer/doctor and knife freak. Cover the front of your magnetic rack with a strip of chamois leather. The other knives will hold it in place and there'll be no more scratching.

CUTTING BOARD

....

THE BUTCHER'S BLOCK is made from dozens of blocks of wood set on end and bound together. This means that the cleaver or knife bites into the yielding 'end-grain' of the wood, which gently parts – protecting the blade edge – and then self-heals. It is often assumed that wooden cutting boards are out of favour with regulators for reasons of hygiene but actually this is not true.* However, in a commercial kitchen, colour-coded boards make it much easier to control cross-contamination and the polypropylene material of which they're made means they can make dozens of trips through a scalding dishwasher.

The traditional Chinese cutting block is circular and thicker in cross-section than the ones we're used to. Western chefs rarely cut parallel to the board and if they need to – perhaps for filleting fish or the very last slice of bread – they must pull their board to the very edge of the table so there's space for their knuckles. With a thicker board, the Chinese chef can flip the *cai dao* and cut horizontally as easily as vertically. Watch a Chinese chef at work and you'll see a lot of horizontal cutting. This may be why the Western knife roll features more flexible knives which can be bent to make a horizontal cut.

Glass, marble or stone cutting boards are... well, I hope you know enough about knives now to understand that anything on which you can sharpen or hone a blade is going to do immeasurable damage when cutting directly into it.

Use an end-grain wooden cutting board if you can, polypropylene if you must, and keep it clean. Best of all, cut lovingly and gently so the knife edge touches the surface with as little trauma as possible.

Love your knife. It will love you back.

---

* 'There isn't any strong evidence that one type of chopping board is more or less hygienic than another, whether plastic, wooden, glass or even marble. What is important is that the board gets cleaned properly after every use and is replaced if it gets damaged, for example from deep cuts or scoring, because this will hinder proper cleaning. You can also stop germs spreading by having separate chopping boards for raw and ready-to-eat foods.' Food Standards Agency (food.gov.uk)

ACKNOWLEDGEMENTS

Tim Hayward

Thanks to the knifemakers, chefs, collectors and geeks who shared knowledge, knives and enthusiasm.

Particular thanks to Jon Warshawsky, James Ross-Harris and Richard Warner from Blenheim Forge, Jay Patel and Rishit Vora from the Japanese Knife Company. To Joshua Heaton, possibly the best edge-man in London at the moment, and to Henry Harris whose vast knowledge, erudition and willingness to teach would surely, in any more civilised culture, have us revering him as a sage.

Thank you to my ever accommodating butcher and advisor Jon West, and Dr Annie Gray for rigorous debate. Though we've never met, I'd like to thank Jose Grant Crichton (née Gilpin) who entrusted me with the family treasure of her father Nat's knives, and to Scott Grant Crichton who facilitated the loan. Amidst all the spectacular knives we featured, Nat's were the most inspiring to have in your hand.

Thank you to Helen Lewis, Laura Willis, Verity Holliday, Emily Noto and Gemma Hayden at Quadrille and my eternally excellent agent Tim Bates.

Thank you to the Home Team, Al, Lib and the crew at Fitzbillies, who continue to put up with my grumpiness and absence, book after book.

Special thanks to Simon Davis who squeezed in time amongst the thrills of new fatherhood to edit brilliantly.

Any illustrated book is a team effort far more wide-reaching than the credits can describe, a bit like traditional Japanese knives made by a group of craftsmen – but I'd like to think this one is more so than usual. It's been a collaboration in which every individual has genuinely added an enormous amount to the scope of the finished project. Thank you to:

Chie Kutsuwada

Chie Kutsuwada, Manga maker, who made some crazily loose ideas into solid brilliance.

Will Webb

Will Webb whose sophisticated, ice-cool design work mirrors his hitman calm.

Chris Terry

Chris Terry whose ability to see as much beauty in a battered old object as a pristine piece has genuinely expanded the remit of this book beyond all our expectations.

Sarah Lavelle

Finally to Sarah Lavelle, who brought us together, led us through and whose name, if anyone's, should be on the blade.

They are *shokunin* all.

INDEX

Page numbers in *italics* refer to illustrations

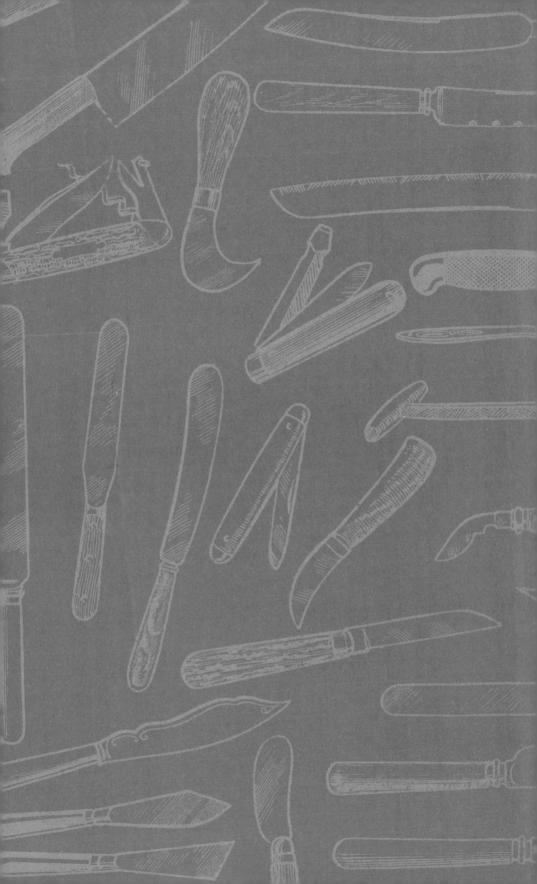